Collins

Student Book 1
Fully revised 4th edition

Your Life

The whole-school solution for PSHE and Citizenship

T0340463

John Foster and Simon Foster

Published by Collins
An imprint of HarperCollins*Publishers*
The News Building
1 London Bridge Street
London
SE1 9GF

HarperCollins Publishers
Macken House,
39/40 Mayor Street Upper,
Dublin 1,
D01 C9W8
Ireland

Browse the complete Collins catalogue at
www.collins.co.uk

11

ISBN-13 978-0-00-759269-2

John Foster and Simon Foster assert their moral rights to be identified as the authors of this work.

British Library Cataloguing in Publication Data
A Catalogue record for this publication is available from the British Library.

Commissioned by Letitia Luff

Edited by Vicky Leech

Managed by Caroline Green

Designed and typeset by Jordan Publishing Design Limited

Copy-edited by Donna Cole

Proofread by Nigel Rumble

Indexed by Jane Henley

Cover design by Angela English

Cover photograph © Shariff Che Lah/Dreamstime

Production by Rachel Weaver

Printed and bound in the UK using 100% Renewable Electricity at CPI Group (UK) Ltd

Contents

Introducing *Your Life*

Your Life Student Book 1 is the first of three books which together form a comprehensive course in Personal, Social and Health Education (PSHE) and Citizenship at Key Stage 3. The table shows how the topics covered in this book meet requirements of the National Curriculum for Citizenship at Key Stage 3 and provide a coherent course in PSHE for students in Year 7.

Personal, Social and Health Education

Personal wellbeing – Understanding yourself and handling relationships	Social education – Responsibilities and values	Keeping healthy
These units concentrate on developing your self-knowledge and your ability to manage your emotions and how to handle relationships.	These units concentrate on exploring social issues and on developing an understanding of your responsibilities towards other people in society, your values and your opinions.	These units are designed to help you take care of your physical and mental health.

- **You and your feelings**
  – anxieties and worries

- **You and your time**
  – managing your time

- **You and your family**
  – getting on with others

- **You and other people**
  – bullying

- **You and your achievements**
  – reviewing your progress

- **You and your responsibilities**
  – beliefs, customs and festivals

- **You and your values**
  – right and wrong

- **You and the media**
  – the power of television

- **You and the community**
  – being a good neighbour

- **You and your opinions**
  – how to express your ideas

- **You and other people**
  – people with disabilities

- **You and your body**
  – growing and changing

- **You and your body**
  – smoking

- **You and your body**
  – eating and exercise

- **You and your body**
  – drugs and drugtaking

The various activities within each unit provide opportunities for you to learn how to grow as individuals, for example, by developing self-awareness and taking responsibility for keeping healthy and handling your money. The group discussion activities involve you in learning how to work as a team and how to develop the skills of co-operation and negotiation. You are presented with situations in which you have to work with others, to analyse information, to consider moral and social dilemmas and to make choices and decisions.

Citizenship

Becoming an active citizen	Economic and financial capability
These units focus on the society in which you live, on its laws and government and on developing the skills you require to become an active citizen.	These units aim to help you to manage your money effectively, to learn about the world of work and to practise the skills of being enterprising.

- **You and the law**
  – why we have laws

- **You as a citizen**
  – how Britain is governed

- **You and the law**
  – children's rights

- **You and global issues**
  – resources, waste and recycling

- **You and the community**
  – taking action

- **You and your money**
  – pocket money, budgeting and saving

- **You and the world of work**
  – attitudes to work

- **You and your money**
  – you as a consumer

- **You and the world of work**
  – developing a product

Anxieties about school

It's natural to be nervous when you start at a new school. Everything seems strange at first. You're unsure where you should go, and what to do if something goes wrong.

Settling in

There are a number of things you can do to help yourself settle in at your new school.

1 Learn the layout. Don't rely on finding your way around by just following the person in front of you. Look at your plan of the school and work out how you're going to get from one classroom to the next.

2 Keep calm. If something goes wrong, don't panic. The thing you probably dread most is making a fool of yourself in front of the rest of the class. If it happens, try to see the funny side of it.

3 Think ahead. Each evening make a list of all the things you need to pack in your bag. Before you leave next morning look at the list to check that you've got everything you need.

4 Study the school rules. If you get to know the rules quickly, you can avoid getting into trouble unnecessarily.

5 Check out what to do in a crisis. Find out who you should tell about things that go wrong. Depending upon what's happened it might be a teacher, the school secretary or a senior pupil.

6 Share your worries. If you're really worried about something, don't keep it to yourself. Ask your form tutor if you can see them privately, or tell your parent(s) what's worrying you.

In pairs

1 Study a copy of the plan of your school. Then take it in turns to test each other about how to get from one place to another. See if you can describe the route without looking at the plan.

2 Study your timetables and help each other to draw up a weekly chart listing the things you need to bring to school on different days of the week.

3 Go through the school rules and write down the answers to these questions:
  a Which places are out of bounds?
  b What rules are there about leaving the premises during school hours?
  c What rules are there about wearing school uniform?
  d What items are not allowed to be brought to school?
  e What kinds of behaviour are not acceptable in school?
  f What rules are there about detentions and other punishments?

Students with problems

1. I feel too ill to go to my next lesson.

2. I've lost my school jumper.

3. I've forgotten to bring my dinner money.

4. I accidentally broke a window.

5. I've come in late and missed registration.

6. The History teacher keeps picking on me.

7. I forgot to tell my parents I'm staying after school for a play rehearsal.

8. I'm having problems with all the homework I get.

In groups

Discuss what each of the students with problems (see above) should do. Which of these people should they report their problem to – form tutor, year head, school secretary, prefect or senior pupil, someone else?

Terry's story

Terry had been at a small primary school in his village with 100 pupils. Mrs Joyce, the head teacher, taught him for most of his subjects and he had enjoyed school and done well.

Now he was in a school of 1000 students and he was taught by 9 teachers in several different buildings. Everyone seemed to be hurrying from place to place and Terry found it very bewildering.

To make matters worse, there was no one from his old school in his class, and the person he was paired with was only interested in football, which Terry knew nothing about.

He began to dread going to school. He didn't want to tell his parents about it, because he felt he was letting them down. He had been excited about starting secondary school, now he felt miserable.

In groups

Discuss Terry's problem. Should he talk to someone about it – a friend from the village? A teacher? Someone in the family? If you were the person he chose to talk to about his problems, what would you say to Terry?

Manjit's story

Manjit was worried about giving a talk to the class. She was shy and hardly spoke at all in group discussions and never volunteered an answer in class, unless the teacher asked her directly.

When it was her turn to give her talk, she was a bundle of nerves. The teacher had told the class that one way of starting was to begin the talk by telling a joke, so Manjit had decided she would do so. But when no one laughed, she got flustered. She couldn't remember what she was going to say next. She just stood there, until the teacher told her to go and sit down.

The teacher kept her after class. She told Manjit how she had had the same thing happen to her when she was at college. She persuaded Manjit to try again.

This time it went much better. Although she forgot parts of it, it was clear that the class was interested in what she had to say about being a refugee. Two of them even asked questions. The teacher was pleased with Manjit and she was pleased with herself for having faced up to her fear and overcome it.

Overcoming anxiety

In groups

Read Manjit's story. Discuss her anxieties and how she overcame them.

In pairs

Here are some other pupils talking about their anxieties at school:

"I don't like having to do role plays in front of the class in drama lessons."

"I worry about what'll happen if I do the wrong thing during a science experiment."

"I'm clumsy and I'm always anxious that I'll make a fool of myself during PE."

Discuss the advice you would give these pupils to reassure them and to help them deal with their anxieties.

Role play

Work in pairs. One of you is someone, like Manjit, who is anxious about having to give a talk to the class. You say that you are going to stay away from school on the days when you might be asked to give the talk. The other person tries to persuade you to face up to your fears and offers advice on how to cope with your anxiety.

Dealing with your feelings

Don't bottle up your worries. Getting advice on how to cope with whatever is bothering you can help you to deal with your problems. Here are three letters from worried young people, and some advice given to them.

I feel rejected

Coping with rejection

I feel rejected. My best friend from primary school is in another class and she's made friends with another girl. We always used to meet up after school and at weekends. Now she's made it clear she doesn't want me around any more. She says I'm boring and she's not interested in the things I want to do. What have I done wrong?

You haven't done anything wrong – It's a shock when you find that you no longer have much in common with someone who's been your best friend. As you grow up, you'll find that people's interests change. Try and stay on friendly terms with your old friend if you can and find new friends that you do have things in common with. But don't try to hang on to her friendship if she's made it absolutely clear she wants no more to do with you. Getting dumped by a friend is always hurtful, but it's not the end of the world.

I've no confidence

Coping with shyness

I've always been quite shy – in fact all my family are pretty quiet – but now it's causing me problems. I never join in with anything and everyone seems to have more fun than me. How do people think of funny things to say? When someone speaks to me I just put my head down because I'm so shy. I've no confidence.

There's nothing wrong with being shy. It's hard, being so self-conscious that you can't join in with others or enjoy yourself. You need to stop imagining that everyone is watching you, waiting to criticise, laugh, find fault – they're not. Most people are too wrapped up in worrying about themselves to bother about others, honest!

The next time someone speaks to you, fight the impulse to turn away. Meet their eyes, smile and listen to what they're saying. Each day, practise chatting to someone new – a teacher or the kid next door. Slowly, you'll grow in confidence. You can do it – starting from now.

I can't get over my grandad

Coping with grief

My grandad died six months ago. We were very close, because he only lived round the corner and I used to see him almost every day. I miss him so much. He was the only person I could talk to about my problems. He'd always listen. I've tried to be strong, but I still get very upset and tearful when I think of him.

At first my parents were sympathetic and helped me to cope with my feelings but now they get irritated with me. I even heard them talking about me to my auntie. She said it was about time I stopped moping and pulled myself together.

Please help me. I don't know what to do. I feel so miserable.

It takes time to get over the death of someone close to you. At first, people understand and offer support, but after a time you might be expected to come to terms with the loss and move on. This, as you've found out, is not always possible, and dealing with grief alone can be very hard.

Don't be too hard on your parents – I'd guess that your sadness brings their own pain to the surface at a time when they are trying to move on too.

You may be lucky to have caring friends, but talking to an outsider may help too – call the CRUSE Bereavement Care Helpline on 0844 477 9400 for support and understanding. CRUSE can arrange counselling to help you face your grief and come to terms with it.

In groups

Discuss the problems these three young people are having and the advice that is given to them. Talk about what you learn from the advice about how to deal with rejection, grief and shyness.

Packing up your cares and woes

If you feel you really can't cope with anything, you're tearful, can't sleep or are distracted all the time, it's time to talk to someone about it.

It may be because of schoolwork, being bullied at school, your health or weight, or a problem that you think someone close to you, like a friend, has and which you don't feel you can help with by yourself.

When you bottle things up even the smallest worries can get blown up out of all proportion and become major problems. Often a worry can be sorted out quickly or simply with a little help from someone else.

They say that a worry shared is a worry halved. And while no one wants to go around moaning about things all the time, anything that is causing you lots of concern should be shared with a sympathetic ear. There may be an easy or fast solution which you haven't thought about but someone with a bit more experience can see immediately.

Your mum and dad are often the best people to help you. If the problems are at home, or you don't feel that you can talk to your parents about it, then your GP, or a friend's mum may be able to help.

Tell them that you are feeling very worried by something and ask if you could talk to them about it for a few minutes when you can be alone. Tell them how worried you are – for instance, if you can't sleep or think about it all the time. Sometimes just talking about things helps. Sometimes you or whatever you're worried about needs more work. Obviously some things like exams or going into hospital can't be helped. It would be unusual not to be a bit worried about these things. Whatever it is, talking to someone who listens and can reassure you is better than suffering in silence. And it's the first step to getting it sorted out.

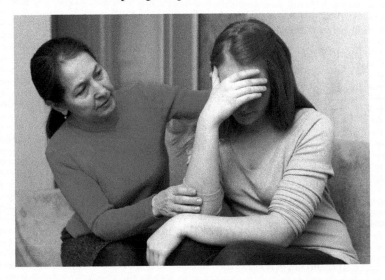

In pairs

Discuss the advice above about sharing your worries. Do you agree with it? Does sharing your worries always help? Is sharing your worries sometimes very hard to do? Talk about why it is sometimes difficult to share your worries.

Tell each other any stories you are willing to share about times when telling someone about your worries has helped you.

In groups

Talk about people you could share your worries with – a parent or guardian, a friend's mum or dad, a teacher, a doctor, a religious person such as an imam or priest or a social worker.

Discuss who you would talk to if you were worried about something to do with: **a)** your parents; **b)** a brother or sister; **c)** a friend; **d)** your school work; **e)** the way someone is treating you at school; **f)** your body.

For your file

Write a story about somebody whose worries get on top of them. In your story, show how sharing their worries with someone helps them to deal with their anxiety.

Growing up

The stage during which a person's body changes from a child's into an adult's is called puberty. Puberty usually starts earlier in girls than in boys. The changes that happen during puberty are caused by an increase in the levels of the female sex hormones oestrogen and progesterone.

In groups

Read the article 'Becoming a woman' and discuss these questions:

1 What is puberty?

2 What causes the changes that happen to a girl during puberty?

3 At what age is it normal for a girl to go through puberty?

4 List the changes that happen to a girl's body during puberty.

Am I normal?

"I seem to be getting left behind by my friends. They all seem to look so much more grown-up than me. I've hardly started to develop at all – I've got a bit of underarm hair, but that's about it."

Christy (13)

For your file

Study the information on this page and draft a reply to Christy.

Becoming a woman

The age at which you develop from a girl into a woman varies from person to person. So there is no right age at which you will go through puberty. Most girls start to develop between the ages of ten and twelve, but some may start at eight and others may not start until they are fourteen. It's important to remember that whatever age you start at is quite normal.

For most girls the first sign of change is that your breasts grow bigger. Your hips and thighs become more curvy and your shape becomes more adult. You will probably also grow taller and you will grow more pubic hair and hair under your armpits.

Around puberty you may produce a whitish discharge, which is nothing to get worried about. Soon afterwards you may have your first period. A girl becomes sexually mature during puberty, and your period along with other changes are a sign that your body's reproductive organs are starting to develop. But it may not come until some time later. Your periods are likely to be irregular for the first year or two, before you settle into a regular monthly cycle.

The changes that happen to your body don't come in the same order for each person. Every girl is different, and you will develop into a woman at your own pace. Don't keep comparing yourself to your friends and expecting things to happen in exactly the same way. It's perfectly normal for some girls to develop earlier than others.

Becoming a man

During puberty your body changes from that of a boy to that of a man. Your weight almost doubles, and your height increases. However, no two boys change in precisely the same way, or at the same age.

As you develop into a man you will grow body hair, and your voice will become deep (break). You may find this embarrassing, because one minute you may have a deep voice, and the next your voice will be high and squeaky. What you look like depends a lot on what your parents look like and the genes you inherit from them. If your father has a lot of body hair, then you probably will as well. Bodies also differ depending on the way they are treated – whether with a diet of nutritious food or junk food, for example.

Puberty is the time of life when a boy starts to become sexually mature. Your reproductive organs develop, and your testes start producing sperm. Your body begins a phase of growth and change in shape that will continue until the late teens.

Puberty is triggered by a hormone, released by the pituitary gland in the brain. This stimulates the testes to release the male sex hormone, testosterone, which controls the changes happening to your body.

Every boy is different, and physical changes in some boys may start at age 12 while other boys will develop even later. Many boys worry that they are developing too slowly or too quickly. It is easy to tease someone because they are bigger and hairier, or smaller and less hairy, than everyone else. However, everyone will eventually go through the same changes, although no two boys will look exactly the same.

In groups

Read the article 'Becoming a man' and discuss these questions:

1 Why are different people's bodies different shapes?

2 What changes happen to a boy's body during puberty?

3 What causes the changes that happen to a boy's body during puberty?

4 At what age is it normal for a boy to go through puberty?

Puberty problems

Organise a questions box (a sealed cardboard box with a slit in the top) into which people can put written questions asking for further information about the changes that occur during puberty and about what is normal.

Getting in touch with your feelings

As your body changes, so too do your feelings. Claire Patterson explains that it's important to understand your feelings.

Feelings can have a big effect on you

They can make you want to laugh, shout, cry or curl up by yourself. Learning to understand your emotions is important. It is like knowing you need to rest when you are tired, eating when you are hungry or putting on warm clothes when you are cold.

Sometimes it's difficult to work out why you have a feeling

Sometimes it's easy to know why you have a feeling and sometimes it's hard. You might be feeling grumpy one evening and not know why. The reason only becomes obvious later. You realise that all evening your parents were fussing over your younger brother and ignoring you.

There is always a reason for having a feeling

It is important to remember that just because you can't always work out why you feel something it doesn't mean there isn't a reason for it.

Always pay attention to your feelings

Sometimes it is difficult to know whether to pay attention to a feeling or not. But it's important to pay attention to feelings that tell you something isn't right. For instance, feeling scared, suspicious, anxious or uncomfortable about someone or something usually makes you want to get away. So it's a good idea to do just that. Your feelings are like your own personal radar so it pays to listen to what they are telling you, even if you are not sure why.

Your feelings can help you sort things out

Your feelings can help you solve problems and make decisions if you learn to pay attention to them. Often, when you find out the facts, you will realize that you were right to listen to your feelings.

Letting your feelings out is good for you

Letting your feelings out is a way of unloading the stresses and strains of things that are affecting you badly. For instance, if something is making you really angry you could try going off by yourself and shouting, thumping a cushion, writing down your angry feelings, painting a big angry picture, or finding someone you trust and talking to them about it.

The stresses from storing up feelings all the time can actually make you physically ill. Bottled-up feelings can also make life difficult for you and others. They may come spilling out at the wrong time and be directed at the wrong person.

Taking care of your feelings

Just as there are ways of taking care of your body, so there are ways of taking care of your feelings. Learning to do this is important if you want to feel strong.

It's important to act on your feelings

There are all sorts of times when people ask you to do things you don't want to do that are perfectly fair – like being asked to dry the dishes or to tidy up your room. There are other times when you have the right to say no if you don't want to do something.

Saying no isn't always easy, especially if you are worried that the other person won't like you if you say no, and you are being pressured into saying yes.

Practice makes it easier

If you practise saying no about little things you will find it easier to say no when it is really important.

How you say no is important too. It helps to say it clearly and firmly. Sometimes it also helps to say how you feel – this makes it clear why you don't want to do something.

If you say yes when you really didn't want to do something, then you are likely to end up feeling anxious, grumpy or resentful.

It takes time and practice to stand up for how you feel

Here are some basic rules:

1 Feelings are real, not imaginary.

2 There is always a reason for how you feel.

3 Following your feelings when you make decisions is always best for you in the end.

Changing feelings and thoughts

During puberty, boys and girls think about lots of new things and feel lots of new feelings:

- You may feel more emotional – up and down.
- You may feel like being on your own more often.
- You may feel awkward and clumsy.
- You may become more attracted to other boys and girls in a different way from before.
- You may start to have heroes and heroines – older people you really admire and try to copy.
- You may feel like dressing like older kids do.
- You may want to spend time with older kids.
- You may feel like being more independent.
- You may find it harder to get on with your parents.

All these things are a usual part of growing up.

In pairs

Study what Claire Patterson says about your feelings and make a list of the most important points she makes. Then show your list to another pair and discuss what you learn from the article about how to manage your feelings.

In groups

Discuss these statements about feelings and give the reasons why you agree or disagree with them:

"Boys who show their feelings and cry are weak. They should learn to be tough and always try to be cool."

"If people really want you to do something with them, the right thing to do is to join in, even if you feel strongly you don't want to."

"There are times when it's best to bottle up your feelings."

"It's often very difficult to explain to someone why you feel the way you do."

Role play

In pairs, role play scenes in which someone says no because they don't feel like doing something. Take it in turns to be the person saying no. Here are some possible scenes:

1 A friend wants you to go to a club.

2 A friend wants you to skip school.

3 A friend asks you to lend them your new DVD.

What do you believe?

What you believe will depend on your cultural background and how religious you are. If your parents are religious, they may have taught you about their beliefs. Many families lead their lives according to the teachings and traditions of a religion such as Christianity, Islam or Hinduism. Your religious beliefs may affect your life in a variety of ways, such as the foods you eat, the clothes you wear and whether or not you have your hair cut.

I believe …

Study the list of statements (below). Use a 5-point scale to decide how strongly you agree or disagree with each statement:

1	2	3	4	5
strongly disagree	disagree	don't know/not sure	agree	strongly agree

Write your scores on a piece of paper.

I believe

1 ... in God.

2 ... that you should pray five times a day.

3 ... that you should not harm or kill any living creature.

4 ... that people who lead wicked lives will go to hell.

5 ... that men should not cut their hair and beards but allow them to grow.

6 ... that you should not eat meat products and dairy products at the same time.

7 ... that women should always keep their legs covered up.

8 ... that you should fast at certain times of the year.

9 ... that you should never gamble.

10 ... that you should not take part in any form of military service.

11 ... that you should only eat fish on Fridays.

12 ... that everyone should give one-tenth of their money to charity.

13 ... that you should take your shoes off before entering a holy place.

14 ... that you should never drink alcohol.

15 ... that you should not work on the Sabbath day.

16 ... that you should never give or receive a blood transfusion.

In groups

Compare your scores for each question. Where you have different scores, discuss why.
Talk about how people from different religious communities have different beliefs. Then appoint a spokesperson and share what you have learned from this activity with the rest of the class.

Dress customs

People may dress differently from you, because of their beliefs. It is important to respect their beliefs and to allow them the freedom to wear what they want without poking fun at them.

In groups

Discuss the views on banning religious symbols and clothing in schools. Would you support a ban in British schools?

In France, the wearing of religious symbols or clothing is banned in schools. Muslim pupils are not allowed to wear the hijab (headscarf), Sikhs are not allowed to wear the dastaar (turban), Jewish children are not allowed to wear yarmulkes (skullcaps) and Christians are not allowed to wear large crosses.

"I would be outraged if there was a ban in the UK on Sikh children wearing turbans."

"I don't see what the fuss is about. People should be able to wear what they like."

"The hijab should be allowed in schools due to freedom of religion and expression."

"The burkha should be banned because it is a symbol of the oppression of women."

"Telling women who choose to wear the burkha that they cannot wear it is oppression itself."

Freedom from discrimination

In October 2009, a Sikh policeman who was ordered to remove his turban to do riot training, was awarded £12,500 compensation by an employment tribunal.

PC Gurmael Singh claimed religious and racial discrimination after being told he must wear a helmet to do the training.

PC Singh joined the police force in 2004. He stated that he is a practising Sikh and it is against his religion to remove his turban in public or to modify it.

In groups

Discuss PC Singh's story. Do you think it was right that he should receive compensation?

Food customs and beliefs

Many religions have beliefs and customs about what foods you should eat. It is important to understand the different religious beliefs about foods and to respect them.

Jewish food laws

Jewish people have laws not only about which foods they may eat, but also about how animals must be slaughtered and how the food is to be prepared, cooked and eaten. Here are some of the main food laws:

1 All food must be prepared according to the law. Such food is known as kosher food.

2 Only meat from animals which have cloven hoofs and which chew the cud, such as cattle and sheep, can be eaten. Meat from animals such as pigs and rabbits is forbidden.

3 Certain birds may be eaten, but meat from birds of prey is forbidden.

4 They can eat meat only from birds and animals which have been slaughtered in a certain way to ensure that all the blood drains out of the body.

5 Meat products and dairy products must not be eaten at the same meal.

6 Dishes and utensils used for meat and dairy products must be kept separate and washed up in separate bowls.

There are special shops that sell only kosher food.

Role play

Study the information about Jewish food laws. Then, without looking at the book, role play a scene in which a teacher is answering a pupil's questions about the foods Jewish people can and cannot eat. Take it in turns to be the teacher.

Salim comes to tea

Jason was delighted when his friend Salim finally agreed to come to tea. They were in the same class and they both went to football practice. They got on really well together.

So Jason had been a bit surprised when Salim had seemed reluctant to accept his invitation.

When he told his Mum that Salim was coming to tea, she said she'd cook something special. But things didn't go at all as Jason and his Mum hoped they would. Salim didn't touch his pork chop, though he ate all the chips and peas.

Afterwards, he didn't go up to Jason's room. Instead, he just said he'd got to be going. He thanked Jason's Mum politely and left. Jason couldn't understand. It wasn't like Salim at all.

It was only later that evening that Jason and his Mum realised what had gone wrong. His Mum was telling her sister Auntie Sarah about it.

'Well, what did you expect?' said Auntie Sarah. 'Salim's family are Muslims, aren't they? I've seen them outside the mosque. Muslims don't eat pork. It's against their religion.'

In groups

Talk about what went wrong when Jason asked Salim to tea. Who was responsible for the misunderstanding? Should Jason have asked Salim whether there were any foods he didn't eat? Should Salim have explained to Jason that he was a Muslim and didn't eat certain foods? Could Jason's mum have done anything to avoid what happened? What do you think Jason and Salim should do now?

Appoint a spokesperson to report your views in a class discussion.

For your file

Muslims try to live their lives according to Allah's laws as laid down in the Qur'an. Actions that are lawful are called halal and actions that are forbidden are called haram. Use the library, resources centre or internet to prepare a factsheet about Muslim food laws, explaining which foods are halal and which are haram.

Festivals

Festivals and celebrations are often based on religious beliefs.

Easter

Easter Sunday is very important for Christians, because they believe that it is the day on which Jesus rose from the dead. Christians all over the world attend church for special Easter services, then have a family celebration at which children are often given presents of Easter eggs. In the past, many Christians gave up certain foods, including eggs, during the period of 40 days before Easter, known as Lent. This may be the reason why eggs have become a special Easter symbol of rebirth.

 **In groups**

What other Christian festivals are there besides Easter? Make a list of them and, on a large sheet of paper, draw up a calendar of Christian festivals. Write brief explanations of the beliefs on which the festivals are based.

Devotees try to form a human pyramid to break a clay pot containing butter during celebrations for Janmashtami in Mumbai.

Janmashtami

Hindus believe that whenever there are troubles in the world, the god Vishnu is reborn in human form to sort them out. At Janmashtami they celebrate Vishnu's rebirth as the religious hero Krishna. Many families put plaster or brass images of Krishna in a cradle which they decorate with flowers. They visit the temple for a ceremony at midnight, the hour of Krishna's birth, when priests bring out a statue of the baby and the worshippers cry out 'Vijay!' which means 'Victory!' The day is then spent celebrating.

In pairs

Choose either a religious festival which one of your families celebrates or a festival from one of the major world religions. Use the library or resources centre and prepare a factsheet explaining the belief on which the festival is based and how people celebrate it. Then, either staple your factsheets together or stick them in a large scrapbook to make a class A–Z of festivals.

How good are you at managing your time?

Do this quiz to find out about how well you manage your time. Keep a record of your answers, and then check what they tell you about your time-management skills.

1 When you make an arrangement to do something, do you write the details on a calendar or in a diary?

a Usually   b Sometimes   b Never

2 When you want to find something in your bedroom, can you find it immediately?

a Usually   b Sometimes   b Never

3 Do you put out the books and equipment you'll need for school next day, and pack your bag, before going to bed?

a Usually   b Sometimes   b Never

4 Do you plan when you're going to do your homework, rather than just doing it when you feel like it?

a Usually   b Sometimes   b Never

5 Do you make sure that you know at what time the buses run, so that you don't spend lots of time waiting at bus-stops?

a Usually   b Sometimes   b Never

6 If someone rings up when you are busy doing something, do you tell them you'll ring them back?

a Usually   b Sometimes   b Never

7 When you have finished using something, do you put it away in the place where it is kept?

a Usually   b Sometimes   b Never

8 Do you waste time each day looking for things because you can't remember where you put them?

a Usually   b Sometimes   b Never

9 Do you plan what TV programmes you are going to watch and fit in your other activities around them?

a Usually   b Sometimes   b Never

10 Do you work out beforehand exactly how you are going to spend the weekend, rather than wait to see what comes up?

a Usually   b Sometimes   b Never

11 Do you always check the opening times before you go somewhere, such as to the shopping centre or swimming pool?

a Usually   b Sometimes   b Never

12 Do you always know exactly what homework you've got each night?

a Usually   b Sometimes   b Never

managing your time

A test-yourself quiz

What your answers say about how you manage your time

Mostly 'a's On the whole you are very good at managing your time. You are organised. You're the sort of person who thinks ahead and plans how you're going to spend your time. You've begun to take responsibility for looking after your belongings, so you shouldn't have to waste a lot of time searching for things. Because you're organised you should be able to fit in your homework and still have plenty of time to do all the other things you want to do.

Mostly 'b's Sometimes you're doing things that make life easier for you, but you're not doing them regularly enough. You need to become a bit more organised in order to make the best use of your time and to help you to stop wasting time. You need to start thinking ahead more and planning how you're going to spend your time. You probably also need to take more care about how you look after your belongings.

Mostly 'c's You're either not too bothered about how much time you're wasting or you haven't yet learned how to organise yourself in order to save time. If you alter your habits, then you'll almost certainly find that you're not getting so stressed and that you've got more time to do the things you like doing. Have a look at the time-saving tips (right) and talk to your tutor and your parents about what you can do to manage your time better.

In pairs

Talk about what you have learned from this activity about how good you are at:

- Organising how you spend your time:
  a) in the evenings; **b)** at the weekend.

- Organising how you look after your belongings.

- Making arrangements with friends and planning activities.

Each make a list of up to three things you could do that would help you to manage your time better.

Time-saving tips

Do you waste a lot of time each day because you forget things you need, or can't find them? Here are some tips to remember:

1. Make lists of the things you need at school each day. Pin them up in your bedroom to remind you.

2. When you've finished using things, always tidy them away.

3. Put things away in the same place every time. Then you'll always know where to find them.

4. Sort out your books and equipment for the next day and pack your bag the night before.

5. Have a folder for important pieces of paper, such as letters about trips. Don't just stuff them in your bag.

For your file

Darren's problem is that he's disorganised and it's getting him down. He wastes so much time that he never has time to do the things he wants to do. Write a letter to Darren, offering him tips on how to manage his time.

How to handle your homework

Four students say what they think about homework and talk about how they cope with it.

Do you think homework is important?

Salima: I think homework is very important. It helps you to understand things, because you have to think things through. It helps you learn what you need to know in order to pass exams.

Tristan: Yeah, I suppose it is. But sometimes it's a waste of time. You feel as if the teacher has only set it because the timetable says it's geography homework every Thursday.

Gary: If you didn't get homework you wouldn't bother to pay attention in class.

Abby: I don't see why we have to have homework. We work hard enough at school as it is. Our evenings should be our own to do what we want.

How much time do you spend on your homework?

Salima: I try to spend as much time as the teachers say you should. My parents won't let me stay up late doing homework. If I haven't finished, they make me stop. Once they wrote to the teacher telling her how long I'd spent on the exercise.

Tristan: It varies. If I'm interested, I might spend a long time on it. Most times, though, I just spend as long as it takes.

Gary: Sometimes I get stuck and it takes me ages and ages, especially when we've got an essay to write. I've been up at ten o'clock some nights trying to get it all done.

Abby: I do it as fast as I can. You're supposed to do an hour an evening, but I never spend more than half-an-hour at the most.

What's the best time to do your homework?

Salima: It depends what else you want to do that particular evening. Sometimes I do my homework as soon as I get in from school. Other times I'll do it later on after I've been to netball practice or drama club, and then had my tea.

Tristan: I do it when I feel like it. Sometimes I forget, then I have to do it on the bus.

Gary: I always do my homework at the same time. I come in from school, watch TV, have my tea, then do my homework.

Abby: I do it in the lunch-hour, or first thing in the morning when I'm waiting for the bell to go. Like I said, I don't see why I should have to do homework anyway.

Where's the best place to do your homework?

Salima: I'm lucky. I've got my own work space in the corner of my bedroom.

Tristan: The best place is somewhere quiet. But it's never really quiet in our house. You can do homework in the library after school if you want, but I'd rather do it at home, even though it's hard to concentrate with my twin sisters about.

Gary: I do it in the kitchen, but it's not ideal. Especially when my dad comes in late from work and wants his tea.

Abby: Anywhere. So long as you can get enough done to keep the teachers off your back.

What do you do if someone interrupts you when you're doing your homework?

Salima: Because I'm in my own room, I don't get interrupted unless someone phones me up. When they do, I tell them I'll ring them back later.

Tristan: It doesn't bother me if I get interrupted. I just go back to it later – or next morning.

Gary: I'm always getting interrupted. I just have to put up with it.

Abby: It's no big deal. After all, it's only homework, isn't it?

Does anyone ever help you with your homework?

Salima: My mum's a doctor, so she sometimes helps me with my science homework. She's really good at explaining things. Once this boy got quite nasty with me because I got higher marks than him and he said I'd cheated. But asking your parents for help is no different from asking the teachers for help.

Tristan: No. My parents are too busy and I'm not that fussed. If I can't do it, I just leave it.

Gary: Sometimes my elder sister helps me, but she doesn't always understand it herself.

Abby: My friend and I often do our homework together. She's better than me at French, so I copy hers, and I let her copy my maths.

In groups

Study what the four people have to say about homework. Talk about the ways that they cope with homework.

- Who has the best homework habits?
- Who has the worst homework habits?
- Who has the least problems with doing their homework well?
- Who has the most problems with getting their homework done?

Talk about where and when you do your homework, and how long you spend on it. Discuss whether anyone helps you and how you deal with interruptions.

Draw up a list of advice on how to cope with homework. Appoint someone to act as spokesperson for your group, then share your ideas in a class discussion.

For your file

Write out a list of Top Ten Tips – How to Handle Your Homework.

Role play

In groups, act out this scene. Three children ask a fourth one to go into town with them. The fourth person refuses because they say they've set aside that particular time to do their homework.

In pairs

Study the list of homework problems below. Note down what advice you would give each person, then share your ideas in a group discussion.

"I never seem to be able to fit it in. I'm always doing it at the last minute."
Aspen

"It seems to take me forever. I never have time to do anything else."
Marsha

"I can never find the books and things I need. I'm always having to go round my friend's to borrow hers."
Martina

"Our flat's very small. There's nowhere I can go to be on my own. I find it very hard to concentrate."
Gregor

"I keep forgetting what homework's been set."
Justin

How should I behave?

As you grow up you will be faced with more and more situations in which you will have to make up your own mind about how to behave. Often you will have to make choices based on your beliefs about what is right and what is wrong.

My ten rules for today

Stefan, aged 12, was asked to write a set of guidelines giving his ideas on what basic rules he thought children should live by. Here's what he wrote:

1 **Don't hurt people or animals** Everyone – and every animal – has the right to live without someone else hurting them.

2 **Don't steal** Society would fall apart if everyone just took what they wanted.

3 **Always tell the truth** Some people say that there are times when it's OK to lie. But I think small lies are likely to lead to big lies.

4 **Don't fight** Fighting never solves anything. It only causes resentment and someone's likely to get hurt.

5 **Don't damage other people's property** If you go around damaging other people's property, you can't complain if they do the same to yours.

6 **Don't be greedy and selfish** Wanting more and more things, and only caring about yourself, causes all kinds of problems.

7 **Take care of the environment** If we don't take care of the environment, we'll destroy it.

8 **Take care of your body** Our bodies are the only ones we've got, so it makes sense to look after them by not doing things like smoking or taking drugs.

9 **Respect other people's opinions and beliefs** I'm not very religious, but some of my friends are. I think it's important to respect other people's beliefs.

10 **Stand up for what you think is right** Don't let anyone bully you into doing things you don't want to do. Always do what you think is right, whatever the consequences.

In groups

Study Stefan's list of rules and his reasons for them. Discuss whether you agree or disagree with them. If you were drawing up a list of rules for today, are there any other rules that you would include? Agree your list of ten rules for today, then choose a spokesperson and share your ideas in a class discussion.

For your file

Write your own guidelines 'My ten rules for today'.

25% of teenagers think cheating is OK

A survey of 10 000 teenagers, carried out for the Money and Morals schools programme, found that 25% thought it was okay to cheat in exams, 22% believed that nothing was wrong in travelling without a ticket and 9% said it was okay to shoplift.

Role play

In groups, role play the following situations. In each situation, half the group wants to do the right thing, while the other half wants to do the wrong thing. Each half must give their reasons why.

1 You are walking past an empty warehouse with a group of friends. There is a sign saying 'No Trespassing'. One of your friends wants to go in and explore.

2 You are at a friend's house when she breaks a valuable vase. She asks you to take the blame.

3 You find a purse with a £50 note in it in a supermarket. You are tempted to not hand it in.

4 A friend asks you to help her cheat in an exam.

5 A friend asks you to lie by saying that he was at your house, when in actual fact he wasn't.

Which is most serious?

In pairs

Below is a list of 12 actions that most people would agree are wrong. Study the list and decide which actions you think are the most serious and which are the least serious. Start by ranking each of them on a five-point scale:

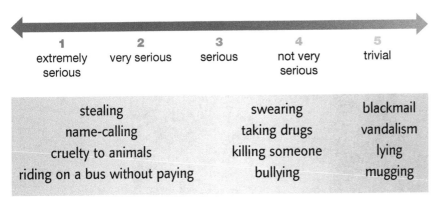

1	2	3	4	5
extremely serious	very serious	serious	not very serious	trivial

stealing	swearing	blackmail
name-calling	taking drugs	vandalism
cruelty to animals	killing someone	lying
riding on a bus without paying	bullying	mugging

For your file

List at least five things you can say to yourself when you are tempted to do something wrong.

Imagine you are speaking in a debate to propose the motion 'It's never right to do the wrong thing.' List at least four reasons to support your argument.

Write about someone you admire because they did the right thing in a difficult situation. Explain why you admire them.

The right thing?

In groups

Read the school essay 'The Right Thing?' (right), which is written by the main character in Robert Leeson's novel *Red, White and Blue*. Discuss what he says about the difficulty of deciding when to tell and when not to tell.

Are people right to despise those who speak up? Discuss the view that it often takes more courage to tell than not to tell.

How to decide what it is right to do

When you are unsure whether it is right to tell, stop and think! Ask yourself these questions:

- What does my conscience say I should do?
- Could speaking up hurt anyone – including me?
- Is it fair to remain silent?
- How would I feel if someone told on me?
- Have I ever been told it's wrong to speak out?
- How will I feel afterwards if I don't speak out?
- What would adults I respect tell me I should do?

English Essay: Own Choice

The Right Thing?

One of the most confusing choices facing a pupil in the first year at school is how to do the right thing and stay out of trouble with your friends and your enemies.

Say something has been stolen. And say your form tutor threatens dire punishment on everyone in the class if it is not returned. Sometimes it is returned in secret and everyone, except the one who has to return it, is happy.

But say they don't. And say you know who has done the stealing? Suppose it is your best friend? Do you tell the teacher?

In one way this is the right thing. On the other hand the worst thing you can do is tell tales, snitch, grass, etc.

Everybody hates the telltale. Even the teachers despise the one who informs.

So the right thing to do might be to tell the person who has done the stealing to put it back, on the quiet. This may work if it is your friend. But suppose it is your enemy, and suppose he or she is bigger than you? Who is going to protect you?

If you tell lies to the teachers, your friends may protect you. But if you tell the truth about your enemy, will the powers-that-be protect you? Can they protect you?

To tell or not to tell?

In groups

Study the list of situations shown right and discuss what you think you should do in each case. Talk about whether it would make a difference to what you would do if the person performing the action is: **a)** someone you dislike; **b)** your friend; **c)** smaller than you; **d)** bigger than you; **e)** younger than you; **f)** older than you. Different people in the group may have different ideas, so be prepared to disagree and to discuss the reasons why you disagree. Keep notes of your views and choose someone to act as a spokesperson so that you can share your views in a class discussion.

For your file

Write your own essay giving your views on what is the right thing to do when faced with difficult situations like the ones you have been discussing.

What should you do if ...?

1 **You see someone taking a chocolate bar from the corner shop without paying.**
Would it make a difference if you knew it was:
a) someone who comes from a poor family
b) someone you know is hungry at school because they often get no breakfast
c) someone who gets lots of pocket money?

2 **You see someone copying someone else's homework.**
Would it make a difference if the teacher has said that who goes into which set will depend on that homework?

3 **You see someone tampering with someone else's bike in the bike sheds.**
Would it make a difference what they were doing, for example:
a) letting down the tyres
b) cutting the brake cable
c) loosening the saddle?

4 **You see someone forging their parent's signature.**
Would it make a difference if it was:
a) a sick note
b) a letter about a detention
c) a report?

5 **You see someone spitting in someone else's drink.**
Would it make a difference if the owner of the drink was:
a) a bully
b) someone who had been spreading rumours about the person who did the spitting?

6 **You see someone tearing pages out of a school text book.**
Would it make a difference if the book was:
a) old and had a torn cover
b) brand new
c) very expensive?

7 **You see someone getting punished for something you know they didn't do.**
Would it make a difference if:
a) you knew who really did it
b) you were the person who did it?

8 **You see someone giving someone else some tablets in the toilet.**
Would it make a difference if you overheard them saying what the tablets were?

9 **You see someone cheating in an exam.**
Would it make a difference if it was:
a) an internal school exam
b) a school entrance exam
c) a public exam?

10 **You see someone claiming something from lost property that you know doesn't belong to them.**
Would it make a difference if the item was valuable?

Mind your manners

Manners are a matter of custom. What are considered good manners in one country may be considered bad manners in another. For example, in Britain belching is regarded as rude. In other parts of the world, it is accepted that people sometimes belch. It is even regarded in some places as a sign of appreciation of a person's cooking. In some societies it is considered bad manners to blow your nose if you have a cold. In others it is considered bad manners to sniff.

In groups

Discuss each of these statements (right) about manners. Decide whether you: **a)** agree with it; **b)** disagree with it; **c)** are not sure, or think that it depends on the circumstances. Talk about the reasons for your views. Appoint someone to take notes and to report your views in a class discussion.

"If there's a queue, you should always join it at the back and wait your turn."

"If a visitor comes into the room while you are watching television, you should always switch it off, even if you're watching your favourite soap."

"When you are talking to an adult you should never use their first name."

"If a bus is crowded and people are standing, you should always get up and give your seat to an elderly person."

"You should never spit, because it's unpleasant and can spread germs."

"You shouldn't swear in public, because many people find it offensive and you should respect their feelings."

"You should never interrupt when someone else is speaking, however much you want to say something."

"You should always put your hand over your mouth if you cough or yawn."

"If you are with other people and you want to eat sweets or crisps, you should always offer them some."

In pairs

'People are less well-mannered than they used to be.' Interview a number of older people and ask them whether they agree or disagree with this statement. Then report their views to the rest of the class.

For your file

Write a statement saying how important you think good manners are. Give reasons for your views.

Table manners

Table manners describe the polite way to behave when you eat a meal at a table with other people. On formal occasions, such as a sit-down meal at a wedding reception, there are certain rules or codes of behaviour called etiquette. These rules are there so that everyone can enjoy sharing a meal together.

Handling cutlery

In most of Britain and western Europe, meals are eaten from individual plates. Handling cutlery (knives, forks and spoons) properly is an important part of table manners.

Hold your knife in your right hand, your fork in your left hand (unless you are left-handed) and cut up your food into bite-sized pieces. Take your time chewing and don't try to swallow large portions or you may choke.

At formal meals, you may find the table is laid with different styles and sizes of cutlery, for example, a soup spoon, fish knife, a dessert spoon and fork (often placed above the plate). Remember to start eating using the cutlery furthest away from your plate and work inwards. Choose fresh cutlery for your starter, main course and dessert.

If you drop your knife or fork on the floor, don't use it again. Get a clean one.

Condiments (seasonings), such as salt and pepper, are usually placed in the middle of the table and passed around, as needed. You may be asked to pass a salt cellar, pepper mill/shaker or a gravy boat.

Table manners worldwide

Table manners and eating habits vary throughout the world. In China and Japan, food is eaten with chopsticks. These are slender, shaped sticks made from ivory, wood or bone. You can eat food quickly from a bowl with a pair of chopsticks, but there are certain rules. It is rude to chew or suck the ends of your chopsticks; don't rest your chopsticks vertically (upright) in food, as this is associated with death. Usually you can place your chopsticks on a special rest, alongside your plate.

In South India, many people use banana leaves as plates and simply throw them away after each meal. Indian and Eastern dishes are often eaten with bread scooped into the food or with fingers. But always use your right hand, never your left hand.

If you follow the rules of basic table manners (right), you should feel comfortable eating a meal anywhere in the world.

A checklist of table manners

Always	Never
✓ Handle your knife and fork with care. Don't wave them around unnecessarily.	✗ Put your knife in your mouth.
✓ Sit upright at the table.	✗ Eat greedily or noisily, or gulp or slurp drinks.
✓ Cut up your food into bite-sized pieces.	✗ Grab food or overfill your plate.
✓ Pass around serving dishes and condiments.	✗ Cough or sneeze over food.
✓ Ask your neighbour politely to pass you anything you want.	✗ Lean across the person next to you to get something you want.
✓ Wait for everyone else to be served before you start eating.	✗ Eat with your mouth open or talk and eat at the same time.

For your file

Study the information about table manners. Then write a letter to a friend who is worried because they have been invited to a wedding where there is to be a formal meal. Offer them advice on how they should behave.

The way other people in your family treat you is affected by the way you treat them. While you have the right to expect them to behave in a considerate way towards you, it is your responsibility to behave in a considerate way towards them.

Problems with parents

When people live together, there are bound to be times when they disagree, so you can expect to have arguments with your parents sometimes.

One complaint that children often make is that, as they grow up, their parents do not allow them enough privacy.

I need my own space

Please help – my mum and dad are driving me up the wall. I'm 11 and have my own room, which would be great if my parents weren't coming in all the time and hassling me. Sometimes I get back from school and all my stuff's been moved around so I can't find anything I want. My mum says she's just tidying up but it really bugs me – she even threw away some old magazines the other day that I'd been saving! I know it sounds horrible but I feel like she's spying on me. My dad's just as bad – he's always coming in and trying to talk to me, when all I want to do is lie on my bed and listen to my ipod. He doesn't even knock before he comes in. I've tried putting 'Keep Out' signs on the door but they just laugh and don't take any notice.

Laura, Manchester

Everyone has a right to privacy, but try to remember it can be hard for your parents to accept that you're growing up and need your own space.

You may find that at first your parents don't really take your need for privacy seriously. It's important that you go about things in the right way, though. Putting up 'Keep Out' signs or accusing them of spying will only annoy them and make you seem childish. You need to explain your point of view calmly but firmly. Tell them that you still love them loads but would just appreciate that bit more privacy now you're getting older.

Show your parents you're growing up by agreeing to take more responsibility for tidying your own room – that way your mum will have less excuse for being in there! It's also a good idea to keep talking to your mum and dad about what's happening in your life. If you're secretive and act like you have something to hide then they'll be more tempted to look around your room to find out what's going on!

In groups

Discuss Laura's problem. Talk about how important it is for each member of a family to have a certain amount of privacy. What do you think of the advice that she is given? Say whether or not you agree with it, and suggest what else she could do to make sure that her parents give her more privacy.

getting on with others

What causes arguments?

In groups

Do you think parents try to control children's lives too much?

1 Why are there often quarrels about clothes? Talk about any arguments you have had about clothes. At what age do you think children should be able to choose their own clothes and decide which ones to wear?

2 Why do parents or carers want to know where you are going and who you are going with? Have they a right to know? At what age do you think you should be able to go out without telling your parents where you are going and who you are going with?

3 Parents often say you must be in by a certain time. Why do they set deadlines? Are they right to want you to come in by a certain time? At what age do you think you should be able to decide for yourself what time you come in?

> **"They buy me what they call sensible clothes. It makes me look so old-fashioned compared to my friends."**

> **"My parents always want to know where I'm going and who I'll be with."**

> **"They insist on me getting home ridiculously early, and if I'm even five minutes late they ground me."**

Doing your share of the chores

Many arguments between children and parents are about the way you behave at home. Parents often say that when you live in a family group, you should expect to have to do your fair share of the household chores. Many children, however, resent doing these chores.

In groups

On your own, copy out the list of household chores (right), and beside each one write down how often you help with that activity: **a)** daily; **b)** two or three times a week; **c)** once a week; **d)** once a month; **e)** hardly ever; **f)** never.

Then, compare how much you help at home with how much other people help. Discuss how much you think children should be expected to help with chores, and whether you think they should be paid for doing so.

Appoint someone to act as spokesperson for your group and share your views in a class discussion.

> Cooking
> Vacuuming
> Dusting
> Cleaning
> Making bed(s)
> Washing up
> Washing clothes
> Household shopping
> Setting the table
> Clearing away
> Ironing
> Gardening
> Cleaning the car

Role play

Choose one of the issues that causes conflict between parents and children and role play an argument about it between a parent and a child. Produce two versions of the role play – one in which the argument develops into a row because the child's behaviour is either angry, sulky or cheeky, and another in which the disagreement is settled because the child remains calm and a compromise is agreed.

For your file

Write a short statement of the reasons why you think children should/should not be expected to help with various household chores.

Top ten tips on how to get on better with your parents

1 **Don't go out of your way to annoy them.** The way your parents treat you may really upset you at times, and it may be tempting to be cheeky or selfish just to get back at them. But behaving childishly never works. It only makes matters worse.

2 **Consider the other people in your house.** Treat the other members of your family in the way you'd like them to treat you. So don't play your music too loud and don't stay on the computer for hours when someone else wants to use it.

3 **Tell your parents things about your life.** Now that you're growing up you'll want more privacy in your life. But they'll still want to know what's going on for you. So keep them informed – they'll be happier if they know what you're up to!

4 **Listen to their point of view.** If there's an argument, make sure you listen to what they are saying and try to understand their concerns. Often they're trying to protect you in some way, even if you feel you don't need that kind of protection.

5 **Let your parents meet your friends.** Don't keep your friends a secret. If they meet your friends and like them, your parents are more likely to trust you when you want to go out with your friends.

6 **Learn to negotiate.** Be prepared to meet your parents halfway over the issues that are causing conflict. For example, you could agree to come in at the time they want you to do in the week, if they'll agree to let you stay out later at weekends.

7 **Don't sulk.** Sulking never works. It can be tempting to lock yourself away in your room sometimes. But your parents will just think you're being immature and won't feel sorry for you.

8 **Give reasons for your viewpoint.** Always try to explain why you feel as you do. Your parents are more likely to take notice of what you are saying if you give them your reasons.

9 **Do your share of the household chores.** You can show your parents that you are growing up by doing your share of the household chores. If they see you being responsible at home, they are more likely to trust you to be responsible when you want to go out.

10 **Never lose your temper.** Even though you might want to scream and shout sometimes, stay calm and take a deep breath. Your parents are more likely to listen to someone who is calm and sensible.

In groups

On your own, study the advice on how to get on better with your parents. Decide which two tips you think are the most helpful. Then form groups and share your views. How useful do you think the advice is? What other advice would you give people of your age on how to get on with their parents? Appoint someone to act as a reporter and share your views in a class discussion.

Getting on with brothers and sisters

Learning to live with your brothers and sisters, in particular to deal with any feelings of jealousy you may have, is an important part of growing up.

"I was really jealous of my big sister, Hayley. She's 15 and everyone goes on about how brilliant she is. She's sitting nine GCSEs, is really pretty and has tonnes of friends and a boyfriend. She's even done some modelling in local fashion shows. No one understands how hard it is for me – I'll never be as perfect as Hayley and people treat me like I'm second best. When I started secondary school all the teachers expected me to be as clever as Hayley and were really disappointed when they discovered I wasn't.

Hayley gets good marks without even trying, while I work like mad and still don't get anywhere. One teacher even told me I wasn't a bit like my sister, like she was a bit disappointed. Sometimes I think that's the way Mum and Dad feel too."

Annabel, 12

Reader's tip:

I used to fall out with my sister all the time. I was jealous of her because I thought she was prettier than me and boys always fancied her. Then one day we had another big row and she burst into tears and said she hated me because I got good grades at school and I'm really sporty. I couldn't believe she was actually jealous of me! We had a big chat and she made me feel really good about myself. Now I realise that everyone has different good points and hopefully me and my sister can help each other.

Ellen, 13

SHOUT TIP: Parents will usually put pressure on their children to do as well as possible – it's because they want what's best for you. Annabel should remember it's other people who are causing problems, not Hayley – in fact, Hayley could well feel pressured by her parents, too.

Annabel needs to tell her mum and dad how she feels and maybe ask them not to pressurise her so much. She could try swallowing her pride and seeing Hayley as a friend, not an enemy. Perhaps Hayley could then help Annabel out with her school work!

Discuss Annabel's problem and the advice she is given. Which piece of advice do you think is the most useful?

Smoking – The Facts

What happens when you smoke?

Tobacco smoke contains over 4,000 different chemicals. When you smoke, these chemicals enter your body through your mouth and throat.

Why is smoking harmful?

Tobacco smoke contains toxic substances – such as nicotine, carbon monoxide and tar – and irritants, all of which affect the way your body works.

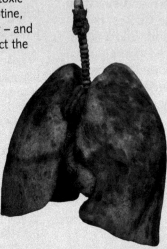

A smoker's damaged lungs.

- **Nicotine** is a very powerful drug which can be addictive. When you inhale tobacco smoke, the nicotine goes into your bloodstream and reaches your brain within about seven seconds. Your blood pressure rises and your heart starts to beat faster.

- **Carbon monoxide** is a poisonous gas that affects the ability of your blood to carry oxygen around your body. Up to 15% of a heavy smoker's blood may be carrying carbon monoxide round their bodies instead of oxygen.

- **Tar** is a complex mixture of chemicals. When you inhale tobacco smoke, tar is deposited in your lungs. Many of the substances in tobacco tar have been shown to cause cancer in animals.

- **Irritants**, which upset the cells in your air passage, are also contained in tobacco smoke. In order to protect the cells, mucus is produced. So smokers start coughing to try to clear the irritants and extra mucus.

Smoking can harm your appearance too

- If you smoke heavily, your teeth may become yellow and stained.

- Your breath often smells of smoke. Your hair and clothes may also smell of smoke.

- Your fingers and nails may get stained by the nicotine.

What diseases does smoking cause?

The main smoking-related diseases are:

- **Coronary heart disease**. This is one of the main causes of death in Britain. Cigarette-smokers are about twice as likely to die from coronary heart disease as non-smokers.

- **Cancer**. 90% of deaths from lung cancer are related to smoking. Smoking has also been linked with the growth of cancer in the mouth, larynx, pancreas and bladder.

- **Chronic obstructive lung disease**. Smoking is the main cause of deaths from bronchitis (inflammation of the mucus membrane of the pair of tubes that branch into the lungs at the lower end of the windpipe) and emphysema (a lung disease where the walls of the air sacs are progressively destroyed).

How great are the risks from smoking?

- People who smoke are more likely to get ill and to die early. 40% of heavy smokers die before retirement age, compared with only 15% of non-smokers.

- Half of the teenagers who currently smoke will die from diseases caused by tobacco if they continue to smoke.

- The greatest risk is of becoming addicted to nicotine. It is estimated that two out of every three smokers either want to give up but can't bring themselves to try, or have tried and failed.

Role play

A friend of yours has started to smoke. Act out a scene in which you try to persuade them to stop. Take it in turns to be the smoker and the non-smoker.

For your file

Using the information on this page, design a leaflet for people of your own age about smoking. Call it 'Ten things you should know about smoking'.

The high costs of smoking

Smoking costs lives

Every year, over 100,000 smokers in the UK die from smoking-related causes.

Worldwide, the number of deaths is 6 million and is expected to rise to 7 million by 2020.

Smoking costs a packet

A person who smokes 20 cigarettes a day will spend over £2,000 a year on cigarettes – enough to pay for a holiday for four people.

Smoking drains the health service

Each year between £3 billion and £5 billion is spent by the NHS on treating smoking-related illnesses.

Smoking damages industry

34 million working days a year are lost because of smoking-related illnesses.

Smoking causes fires

Each year 100 people die and 1000 people are injured in fires caused by smoking.

Smoking damages the environment

Each year an area the size of Tokyo is cleared for tobacco farming. Up to 20 million people could be fed if this land was used for crops other than tobacco.

Tobacco plants are treated with pesticides, which stay in the soil and can pollute rivers.

Drying the tobacco plant produces greenhouse gases that cause global warming.

Smoking exploits people

Although cigarette consumption has fallen considerably in developed countries in recent years, it has increased in the developing countries, which have been targeted by the tobacco companies.

Cigarette advertising is not banned in these countries. There is little regulation in place to raise awareness of the dangers of smoking, or to restrict the sale of tobacco.

Some poorer countries are dependent on the income tobacco production generates for their economies. But the production of tobacco does not create wealth to help them out of poverty. The tobacco companies pay very low prices to local farmers for their crops, while charging them high prices for raw materials such as seed and pesticides.

Stuart's story

My dad died from lung cancer when he was 44. He'd always been a heavy smoker. He said he'd started smoking when he was 12 and wished he never had. I'll never smoke, because I've seen what it can do to people.

In groups

Imagine you have been asked to run an anti-smoking campaign to discourage people of your age from starting to smoke. Plan a 30-second TV advert. Then share your ideas in a class discussion.

What do you really think about Smoking?

Emma, 18, a secretary; Carole, 21, a shop assistant; Kate, 17, a student; and Mike, 19, an apprentice engineer, give their views on smoking issues.

When did you start smoking and why?

Mike: I was 15. Looking back I guess I did it to be part of the in-crowd. I didn't really like the taste and the first few times it made me feel sick and light-headed, but stupidly I carried on.

Emma: I started smoking at 11. I took to it immediately – just really enjoyed it – I suppose it was as much the doing it with friends and feeling grown up as the smoking.

Carole: I began smoking at 19, pretty early compared to my friends. Both my parents are smokers, so there was a sense of inevitability about it. I just really enjoy smoking.

Do you think smoking is glamorous?

Mike: No way. It's unhealthy and smelly. I think it's disgusting – especially when you wake up in the morning and your mouth tastes like an ashtray – but the first thing I do is reach for a fag, so what can I do about it?

Emma: I do think smoking can look good. It doesn't make me want to take it up again, though, because I am now completely turned off by people who smoke.

Kate: I think tobacco ads should be banned. The bottom line is that people die from smoking and we have a responsibility to tell it like it is. People smoke because smoking has been made to look glamorous.

What do you think about passive smoking?

Emma: It's not something I really think about when I am out with a crowd of smokers. But I do get annoyed when I get home from a night out and my hair and clothes stink and my eyes are burning. Also I hate to see pregnant women smoking, that shocks me. Smoking is selfish.

Carole: See, that's what I really hate – people calling us selfish and going on about what a dirty habit it is. This passive smoking is a load of rubbish. We're all going to die one day so what is the point of worrying?

Kate: I don't agree with that at all. I'm in favour of bans in workplaces and other public places. There's plenty of evidence that passive smoking is a killer.

Have you ever tried to stop?

Mike: Yes. I've stopped smoking for months at a time, but I've never given up. Apart from my lungs giving up or the threat of cancer – I don't know if I can stop for good. I just consider myself addicted to smoking and therefore I feel helpless.

Carole: No. I haven't ever tried to stop, even when my boyfriend's dad died of lung cancer. I reckon I'm pretty safe as I'm only a light smoker. Unlike Mike, I can give up if I want to.

Emma: I haven't smoked for three years and I believe I never will. It wasn't easy giving up – the older I got the more addicted I thought I was and the harder it seemed. It was difficult because many of my friends smoked and they seemed to see it as a personal betrayal when I stopped. But we got over that.

In groups

- What do you think are the main reasons why young people start to smoke?
- Talk about passive smoking. How concerned are you about passive smoking?
- What do you learn from the article about how addictive smoking is and how hard it is to stop smoking? What do you think about what Carole says about stopping smoking?

Electronic cigarettes

'If all the smokers in Britain stopped smoking cigarettes and started smoking e-cigarettes we would save five million deaths in people who are alive today.'

Professor John Britton, Royal College of Physicians.

Electronic cigarettes, unlike traditional cigarettes, do not contain tobacco. Instead they contain liquid nicotine. There is a mechanism which heats the nicotine and turns it into a vapour that smokers inhale and exhale. Because they do not contain tobacco, they do not contain tar and the other harmful chemicals in tobacco. But they provide the smoker with nicotine, which is addictive.

Around one million smokers in Britain were smoking e-cigarettes in 2013. However, there is little research into how safe e-cigarettes are and whether smoking them has any long-term effects. E-cigarettes are to be licensed as medicines from 2016.

"Regulation can ensure that adult smokers can buy e-cigarettes, but promotion to children and non-smokers will be prohibited."

Deborah Arnott ASH

In France, smoking e-cigarettes is banned in public places. You have to be over 18 to buy them and firms are not allowed to advertise them.

In groups

1 Was the government right to ban all tobacco advertising and sponsorship?

2 What do you think of the idea that all cigarettes should have to be sold in plain packets? Do you think the current health warnings are effective?

3 Is banning shops from displaying cigarettes on their shelves a good idea? Will keeping them under the counter reduce sales?

4 How effective is the ban on selling cigarettes to under 18s? Should shopkeepers who sell cigarettes to people under 18 be banned from stocking cigarettes?

5 Should people with smoking-related illnesses have to pay for their hospital treatment? Should the tobacco companies be made to contribute to the cost of their treatment?

6 'The best way of stopping people from smoking is to keep on putting up the price of cigarettes, by increasing the tax on them.' Discuss this view.

7 'Smokers have the right to smoke.' Discuss this view. Should pubs be allowed to have separate rooms for smokers?

8 What is your view of electronic cigarettes? Should it be illegal to sell them to children? Should they be banned until more research is carried out into their long-term effects?

9 Should there be a law banning smoking in cars with children in?

Tobacco and the law

- All forms of tobacco advertising and promotion are banned in the UK.

- Cigarette packets must carry a government health warning.

- Smoking is banned in all enclosed public places and workplaces in the UK.

- It is illegal to sell tobacco products to anyone under the age of 18.

- Tobacco products must be hidden in closed cupboards or kept under the counter in large shops and supermarkets. From 2015 this will apply in all shops.

8 You and the law

Why do we have laws?

If there were no laws, people could do what they liked to you and your property. They could break into your home, steal all your belongings and beat you up, without fear of being punished. They could promise to pay you money, if you did some work for them, and then laugh at you when you asked to be paid. They could point a gun at you and make you do something you did not want to do.

Without laws we would live in fear. The strongest or most powerful individual or group of people would control our society. So there is a system of laws to protect you and your rights. The law states what your rights are and what your duties are towards other people. The law also states what the penalties are for anyone who breaks the law. There is a police force to keep order and stop people from breaking the law, and to arrest people who do.

Sometimes a law is introduced which some people think is unfair. These people are protesting about the ban on foxhunting. In a democracy, you have the legal right to protest peacefully and to seek to change the law by lawful means, such as collecting signatures for a petition.

Knowing and respecting the law

It is your responsibility to know what the law says and to obey it. Ignorance of the law is not regarded as a valid excuse if you are found breaking the law.

Each country has its own laws. When you live in a country, you must obey its laws. When you visit another country, you must obey that country's laws.

The majority of people respect the law and obey it. There are a number of reasons why people are law-abiding. They may have strong religious or moral principles. They may be afraid of the punishments they might receive if they are caught and found guilty. They may want to avoid the shame of being labelled a criminal and sent to prison.

In groups

Discuss how your life would be different if there were no laws and why we need to have laws.

What are your legal responsibilities? Why is ignorance of the law not regarded as a valid excuse?

Why do most people obey the law?

Imagine that your year group is shipwrecked on a desert island. No adults are with you. Discuss how you would set about drawing up some rules for everyone to follow until you are rescued.

Things to consider:
- Who will make the rules?
- Who will enforce the rules?
- What rules will you have to ensure personal safety?
- What rules will you have about property?
- How will you settle disputes?
- How will you deal with those who break the rules?

Choose a reporter to note down your ideas and to report them in a class discussion.

'The day the countryside came to town' a march protesting the ban on fox-hunting in London

Civil law and criminal law

Laws can be divided into two types. Laws about crimes, such as theft, vandalism and assault, which the government enforces, are part of what is called criminal law. Laws concerning your private rights, in your dealings with other people, such as borrowing and lending money, are part of what is called civil law.

Solicitors

If you are accused of committing a crime, a solicitor can explain what your rights are and can arrange either to represent you in court or for another lawyer to do so.

A solicitor can also help you in your private matters, such as making a will, buying and selling property, setting up a business and in your dealings with other people. If you have a dispute with someone, who won't pay you for something, or who claims you owe them money, you can ask a solicitor to act on your behalf. The solicitor may be able to settle the matter without it going to court by contacting the other person or their solicitor.

Civil courts

Minor civil cases are dealt with in courts called county courts and important cases are dealt with in the High Court. There are about 400 county courts in England and Wales. Scotland and Northern Ireland have their own court systems.

If your claim is for £500 or less, you can take it to the County Court yourself without needing a solicitor. You can get advice about the small claims procedure from your local Citizen's Advice Bureau or from https://www.gov.uk/make-court-claim-for-money/going-to-court.

Role play

You ordered and paid £300 for a tablet from a company, but it never arrived. The company claimed they delivered it and refused to send you a replacement. Role play a scene in which you and a friend discuss what you should do.

In groups

Discuss the following opposing views:

"Courts are an expensive and time-consuming way of settling disputes. It's always better to settle out of court."

"The only place to settle a dispute fairly is in court."

Neighbours and the law

The law says that neighbours must not interfere with each other's rights to enjoyment of their property. If your neighbour's behaviour is unreasonable, it is best to try to sort it out by speaking face-to-face and calmly working through the issues. This is more likely to resolve the matter than immediately involving the council or taking legal action.

If the nuisance continues this may result in legal action. The case will be heard in a civil court. Damages may be awarded but more often the court will make an order, known as an injunction, telling your neighbour to stop causing the nuisance. If they do not stop, they may be fined or sent to prison.

For your file

Your local council will provide information about what pets you are allowed to keep in council properties and how you must control them. Visit your local council website to discover what the council's rules are. Then write a paragraph summarising what you have found out.

Noise

Noise is one of the most common causes of disputes between neighbours. A certain amount of neighbourhood noise is regarded as acceptable, but if your neighbour plays the trumpet late every night or uses an electric drill regularly in the early hours of the morning, then you have cause for complaint. The noise must be continuous and repeated before you can take your neighbour to court. The Environmental Health Department of the local council advises people about what they can do about noise nuisance from nearby homes and factories. The council may issue a noise abatement notice if the noise is persistent and intense.

If there is a noisy party, you can call the police, who may come and ask for the music to be turned down.

You sometimes need planning permission to run a business from your home. If a business uses noisy machinery, your neighbours might complain. You might have to reduce the noise and you would be in trouble if you did not have planning permission.

Trespassing

You cannot go onto someone's property without permission. If you do so, you are trespassing. So if you kick your football into someone's garden, you can't just climb over a fence to get it back. You must get permission to go into the garden or go and collect it from them.

If the ball causes damage, for example smashes a window, they can ask for you to pay for it and they could take you to court if you didn't.

Signs like this are worded wrongly. Trespass is a civil offence. You can take someone who trespasses on your property to a civil court, but you cannot prosecute them in a criminal court.

Pets and animals

There may be restrictions on whether or not you and your neighbour can keep pets or animals. Even if there are no restrictions, if an animal causes a nuisance, the neighbours can complain, for example, if a dog keeps barking. If you think the neighbour is ill-treating their animals, you can contact the RSPCA. They can prosecute people who treat animals cruelly.

Certain dogs, such as pit bull terriers, have to be registered under the Dangerous Dogs Act and there are plans to register all dogs by microchipping them. You need a licence if you want to keep an exotic or wild animal as a pet.

Bonfires

There is no law preventing anyone from having a bonfire in the garden. But if the smoke from a bonfire causes a nuisance and your neighbour has regular bonfires – which cause pollution by burning household rubbish – you can complain to the local council.

Harassment

Harassment can take a number of forms, such as threats of violence to you or damage to your property, actual damage, verbal abuse, insulting or intimidating behaviour. Harassment is an offence and should be reported to the police. They may warn the offender and if the harassment continues may prosecute them. Cases of harassment are dealt with in the criminal courts.

Antisocial behaviour

Anyone who persistently causes trouble in a neighbourhood can be banned from entering it under an Antisocial Behaviour Order or can be asked to sign an Acceptable Behaviour Contract.

Teenagers issued with ban

Two teenagers who tore round Burnley Hospital on their bikes have been given anti-social behaviour orders. They are banned from entering an area in the vicinity of the hospital unless supervised by a parent or guardian and from associating with each other.

Under the terms of the order, they must refrain from using abusive or threatening language and from harassing local residents or throwing objects with the intention of causing damage, alarm or distress.

If they breach the order, they could be fined or taken into custody.

Adapted from the *Burnley Express*, 21 February 2013

In pairs

What do you think an Acceptable Behaviour Contract should contain? List all the types of anti-social behaviour that a person who is causing trouble in a neighbourhood should have to agree not to do. For example, 'I agree not to empty rubbish bins in people's gardens. I agree not to congregate in the stairwells of the blocks of flats in X street'. Draw up an Acceptable Behaviour Contract that you would give to a troublemaker. Then compare your contracts in a group or class discussion.

In groups

What can I do? Discuss what the law is in these situations. Then write the replies that you would post on the *Ask Erica* website to the people who have e-mailed you asking for advice.

Ask Erica

I kicked my football over the fence and it smashed part of my neighbour's greenhouse. Can I climb over the fence and get it back?   *Virat*

Our neighbour has at least a dozen cats. Her flat stinks and the cats are always trying to get in our house and treat our garden as if it is theirs.   *Sonia*

This boy is harassing an old lady in our street. He calls her names, throws stones at her windows and has threatened my brother when he tried to intervene.   *Vic*

The man next door had a bonfire. He burnt some felt off his garage roof. The smell was awful and the smoke got everywhere.   *Amina*

Our next door neighbour keeps on playing loud music till midnight.   *Gareth*

9 You and other people

What is bullying?

Bullying can take many forms, such as:

- **Physical bullying** – pushing or hitting someone, damaging their things, stealing from them or forcing them to hand over money or belongings.

- **Verbal bullying** – name calling, spreading rumours, nasty teasing, threats, insults. Sending nasty or threatening e-mails or text messages.

- **Emotional bullying** – ignoring or deliberately leaving someone out. Making nasty remarks about someone's family or home life. Always criticising or 'rubbishing' everything they do.

- **Prejudice bullying** – bullying someone because of the colour of their skin, their religion or country of origin. Some people may get bullied because they wear glasses or a hearing aid, or just because they look different.

From the *Kids Aware* website

> "Picking on someone and tormenting them all the time." **Claire**

> "Bullying is making you do things you don't want to do by threatening you." **Jason**

> "A bully is a person who deliberately sets out to hurt someone else." **Khalid**

> "Sometimes teasing is bullying. It depends who is teasing you and what they are teasing you about." **Morgan**

In groups

1 Discuss these comments about bullies and bullying. What is the difference between teasing and bullying?

2 Discuss the different forms of bullying. Are some kinds of bullying more hurtful than others?

3 Draft a short statement giving your group's definition of bullying. Choose a spokesperson to report your views and share them in a class discussion.

Who gets bullied?

There is no such thing as a typical victim. Bullies pick on people for all kinds of reasons. A person may come from a different background or speak with a different accent. They may be picked on because they look different – they wear glasses or a brace – or because they have red hair or dark skin. They may be good at exams or come bottom of the class. They may like the 'wrong' music or wear the 'wrong' clothes. However, the victim is often physically weaker or younger than the people who torment them.

One Direction's Zayn Malik was targeted by online bullies after his cousin uploaded a family photo from a Muslim festival.

Cher Lloyd: It's funny to say "How do you cope?" Because I don't cope with it. It's really hard. If I get a nasty tweet or someone shouts at me in the street, that's really disrespectful to me and my family. I kind of wait until I get home. You shut the door and then you can have a good cry about it. No one needs to know.

Cyber bullying

Cyber bullying is when a person or a group of people uses the internet, mobile phones, online games or any other type of digital technology to threaten, tease or humiliate someone.

What are the different types of cyber bullying?

Email

Sending abusive or nasty emails – including sending emails to a group of people who join in the bullying.

Instant messaging (IM) and chat rooms

Using instant messaging and chat rooms to send threatening or abusive messages to someone and asking others to join in.

Social networking sites

Writing nasty or upsetting comments on someone's profile and making jokes or comments about people on your own status updates or tweets.

Setting up a fake profile dedicated to bullying someone else.

Online gaming

Abusing or harassing someone through multi-player online gaming sites.

Mobile phones

Sending abusive texts, video or photo messages.

I'm being cyber-bullied. What should I do?

- Talk to someone you trust like a parent, carer or teacher.

- Keep a copy of any abusive texts, emails, messages or comments that you receive and record the dates and times they were sent. With cyber bullying there is always a trail and keeping a record can be very useful when you are reporting the bullying.

- Try not to reply to any messages you receive. It can encourage the bullies and end up upsetting you more.

- You can contact a helpline such as Childline for advice. You can talk to Childline on 1-2-1 chat or contact them via their website (www.childline.org.uk) or phone 0800 1111.

In groups

Discuss the different forms of cyber bullying. Are some forms of cyber bullying more serious than others?

Role play

In pairs, act out a scene in which an adult confronts a person involved in cyber bullying. The bully tries to defend their actions by saying it was just a bit of fun but the adult explains to them that it is a very serious matter.

In pairs, act out a scene in which a friend tries to comfort someone who is being cyber bullied and offers them advice on what to do about it.

What does it feel like to be bullied?

Lana's *story*

It all started when a group of us were playing football in the playground. I took a shot at goal and by mistake the ball hit this older girl who was standing watching. It left a big red mark on her face.

She was furious and threatened to get me after school. On the way home she and one of her friends were waiting for me. They pushed me up against a wall and slapped my face.

Since then, they've made a point of picking on me. They barge into me in the corridor and call me names. They've taken my bag off me and tipped the contents all over the cloakroom floor. They're making my life miserable. I lie awake at nights thinking about them and I try to think of places where I can hide at break times so they won t find me.

Stephen's *story*

I used to get picked on a lot at primary school, because I'm very short-sighted and I'm not very good at games. So when I moved to secondary school, I made sure it was quite far away.

I really like my new school, but the bullying hasn't stopped. Because I enjoy studying and get good grades, most of the boys in my class don't like me. They've started to make my life a misery. They call me names and flick towels at me in the changing-rooms. So on P.E. days I pretend I'm not feeling well and try to get my mum to write me a note.

One of them has threatened to beat me up if I don't let him copy my homework. I'm worried the teacher will notice and I'll get into trouble.

There's no one I can talk to about it. If I told my dad, he'd simply say I must learn to stand up for myself.

In groups

Discuss what you learn from the stories and statements on these two pages about what it feels like to be bullied. Do you agree that sometimes mental bullying is worse than physical bullying?

'Text bullies and email bullies are cowards who hide behind their anonymity.' Discuss this view. What advice would you give to someone who is being bullied by mobile phone messages?

Role play

In groups of four, act out a scene in which Stephen is being picked on. Before you begin, discuss the different ways that Stephen could react to the bullying. Repeat the scene a number of times, showing Stephen's different reactions and giving everyone a chance to be Stephen. Then, as a class, discuss what it feels like to be in Stephen's position and decide which reaction is the best way of coping with the bullying.

It hurts

It hurts when someone makes remarks
About the clothes I wear,
About the foods I refuse to eat
Or the way I cover my hair.

It hurts when someone laughs and jokes
About the way I speak.
'Ignore them,' says my dad, but it's hard
To turn the other cheek.

It hurts when someone calls me names
Because of the colour of my skin.
Everyone's different outside
But we're all the same within.

John Foster

For your file

Study the poem. Imagine you are the person in the poem. Write a diary entry about a particular incident in which you were bullied. Describe what happened, how you felt at the time and how you feel about it afterwards.

What should you do if you're bullied?

1 You are on your way to school when a gang of older bullies surrounds you and demands that you give them your dinner money. Do you:

- a Fight them?
- b Shout and run away?
- c Hand over the money and say nothing?
- d Hand over the money, then tell a teacher?

2 You are in the school playground and somebody barges into you. You're not sure whether it's accidental or on purpose. Do you:

- a Push them back hard?
- b Demand an apology?
- c Ignore them?

3 Someone is spreading nasty rumours about you. Do you:

- a Tell a teacher?
- b Start spreading rumours about them?
- c Ignore what's happening?
- d Confront them and ask them to stop?

4 A gang of bullies gets you alone and starts beating you up. Do you:

- a Do nothing – just take it?
- b Fight back?
- c Shout to attract attention?
- d Watch for your chance and run away?

5 Your classmates start teasing you about your appearance. Do you:

- a Pretend it doesn't bother you?
- b Show that you're angry and threaten them?
- c Tell a teacher?
- d Calmly and politely ask them to stop?

6 You're in the toilet when an older pupil comes in and for no apparent reason gives you a punch. Do you:

- a Wait until they leave, then tell a teacher?
- b Get into a fight with him/her?
- c Accept what happened and do nothing?

7 You are going into the dining room at lunch time and someone yells a negative comment at you. Do you:

- a Ignore it?
- b Yell back?
- c Tell a dinner supervisor?

8 You're with a group of friends when they start tormenting someone. You know they will turn on you afterwards if you don't join in. Do you:

- a Join in?
- b Try to make them stop?
- c Stand and watch, but do nothing?
- d Go and find an adult who will stop them?

In groups

Discuss these situations (above) and decide what you think is the best way of dealing with each one. There are no right answers, because every set of circumstances is different. But remember that how the situation develops will depend upon the action you decide to take. Make a note of your decisions and then share your views in a class discussion.

How to beat the bullies

If bullying is getting you down, here's what you can do ...

- Try to ignore the bullies and pretend they aren't winding you up. If they fail to get a reaction, they may give up.
- Try standing up for yourself. Be assertive, but don't come down to their level by joining in fights and slanging matches – you may be the one who ends up in trouble.
- Ask your friends and classmates to stick up for you. If you all stick together, the bullies lose their power.
- Take a class in self-defence – not to help you fight back, but to help boost your confidence.
- Keep a record of what's happened and ask your friends if they'll act as witnesses if you need adult help to sort things out.
- Tell your parent(s) or guardian what's happening.
- Tell a sympathetic teacher about the problem.
- If the bullying doesn't stop, go back to your teacher and explain. Get your mum or dad to help you take the problem to your year head or school principal if necessary.

Stay SMART online

Safe. Keep safe by being careful not to give out personal information – such as your name, email, phone number, home address or school name – to people you don't know or trust.

Meeting someone you have only been in touch with online can be dangerous. Only do so with your parent(s) or carer's permission, and even then only when they can be present.

Accepting emails, IM messages, or opening files, pictures or texts from people you don't know or trust can lead to problems – they may contain viruses or nasty messages.

Reliable. Someone online might be lying about who they are, and information you find on the internet might not be reliable.

Tell your parent, carer or a trusted adult if someone or something is upsetting you or makes you feel uncomfortable or worried.

From Childline. Please find out more at: www.childline.org.uk

In groups

Discuss the advice given in the article.

Do you agree that it is essential to speak out and that speaking out is not telling tales? Give your reasons.

Which three pieces of advice do you think are the most useful?

Dealing with taunts and insults

Fogging

If you respond to insults with more insults, they can build up until they become unbearable. Try 'fogging'.

How it works

When other people make hurtful remarks, don't argue and try not to become upset. Imagine that you are inside a huge, white fog-bank. The insults are swallowed up by the fog long before they reach you. Nothing touches you.

Reply to taunts with something short and bland. 'That's what you think.' 'Maybe.' Then walk away.

This might seem very strange at first and very hard to do, but it does work and it can help you blot out insults.

Practise by thinking of the worst things the bully says to you and pretend that you are inside your fog-bank – nothing reaches you.

In pairs

Discuss what is meant by 'fogging'. Does it strike you as a useful way of dealing with taunts and insults?

A class bullying policy

In groups

Draft a class bullying policy. List all the types of behaviour that you consider to be bullying and, therefore, unacceptable. Explain what procedures someone should follow if they are the victims of bullying. Share your ideas in a class discussion and write out an agreed policy. Then, use a word processor to produce a copy of the policy for everyone to have, and put a copy on the class noticeboard.

Don't suffer in silence

Dear Liz

I'm 14 and I'm not bullied in school, but I get threats from an older girl who goes to my school and lives in my street. We used to be really friendly but we fell out. I get nasty calls on my phone, and takeaways and taxis sent to our house. I know her friends are behind it because I've heard them say things that only she would know. Do you think the school will do anything about her if my mum complains?

Sarah

Hello Sarah

We should always encourage young people to go to their school about bullying issues, whether it is in school, online or outside the school premises. They do have a clear remit to respond to such cases. However, if this is impossible, the police are the best people to help here. If you get any more offensive or threatening texts, don't reply but save them and get your parents to contact the police. Sending these messages can be two types of offence: they might be breaking telecommunications law and if they are part of a campaign against you the callers might be charged with harassment.

If you take your phone to the police, they can find out from your mobile phone company where the messages came from. Another way to stop the problem is to change your mobile phone SIM card.

Liz

Dear Liz

I go to a school with not many pupils from different backgrounds, so I stand out. I'm often called names and jokes are told about me. I'm told to go back where I came from, but this is my home and I was born here. My family don't know what's being said and I don't want to upset them by telling them. They don't speak English very well and they might not be able to sort it out for me.

Jasbinder

Hello Jasbinder

If these ignorant people are making nasty remarks about your background, colour and culture then this is racism and needs to be tackled. Try speaking to your class teacher and getting the school to sort it out. If this doesn't work, then you can contact the police. Many police forces have police–school liaison officers who can be very useful in warning the bullies off.

Bullying problems

A few years ago I was diagnosed with diabetes. Most of my friends are OK, but some of them still take the mick. It can be upsetting. What should I do?   *Darren*

There's a lot of trouble on the school bus. There's this older boy who picks on me and calls me names. The other people on the bus just laugh because they don't want him picking on them. What can I do?   *Thurston*

There are a couple of bullies in my school who are bullying another boy. I feel very sorry for him. He doesn't tell anyone. They steal his money and make him cry. Once they smashed his glasses and put them down the toilet. Is there anything I can do?   *Claire*

In groups

Discuss the advice Liz gives Sarah and Jasbinder. How useful do you think her advice is? Will it help them to solve their problems?

Draft the advice that you think Liz would give to Claire, Thurston and Darren.

Television and its influence

Most young people aged between five and fourteen watch over 20 hours of television each week. What influence does TV have on you? Does it play too big a part in your life? Does it affect your views and values?

"A lot of TV programmes are silly, like cartoons. But you can learn a lot from TV, especially the news and documentaries. It depends what you watch."

"I think people waste a lot of time watching TV when they could be out doing more interesting things."

"I don't think people get their views and values from what they see on TV. I think they get them from their families."

"My grandad says TV has influenced the way people communicate and how they relate to each other. Some people don't even switch the TV off when they have visitors."

"Of course TV influences what you think. That's why advertisers pay so much to promote their products."

"There's too much violence on TV. People say that it doesn't do any harm, but I think it does. You get so used to seeing violent things on TV that when something happens in real life you're not as shocked as you should be."

In groups

Do you agree with these comments made by young people about TV? Discuss each one in turn and say how much you think TV influences you and whether you think it plays too big a part in your life. Appoint someone to act as spokesperson and get them to report your views in a class discussion.

For your file

Write a short statement saying how much influence you think TV has on your views and values, and whether you think it plays too big a part in your life.

A fair picture?

Does television give fair coverage of people from all sections of society? Charlie doesn't think so (see her statement, right).

In groups

Discuss Charlie's statement. Does television present a fair picture of: **a)** older people; **b)** people with disabilities; **c)** people from ethnic minorities?

TV isn't fair

I don't think television presents a fair and balanced picture of society as it really is.

I don't like the way older people are shown. Too often they are stereotyped as being useless and out of touch.

Also, there aren't enough programmes featuring people with disabilities. It's as though they're invisible.

There are now more people from ethnic minorities reading and reporting the news, but there should be more of them in things like soaps and situation comedies.

the power of television

Fact or fiction?

When you are watching TV dramas and soaps, the acting is often so convincing and the setting so realistic that you can easily forget that you are watching a fictional story.

The cast of Hollyoaks 'out of character'

How true to life are soaps?

What the writer says:

The stories I write are based on what I've observed in my own and other people's experiences. So in one sense they are true. But that's as far as it goes. Things don't happen in real life exactly as they do on the screen. For a start, everything happens more quickly on the screen. You only put in the exciting bits. Real life is far more boring and uninteresting than what you see on TV.

In real life people don't talk the way they do in TV dramas. My characters usually express themselves clearly and fluently. In real life people tend to hesitate much more when they speak, to pause, to use lots of 'ums' and 'ers', to not finish their sentences and to repeat themselves.

What the director says:

Our storylines are about the type of events that do occur in people's lives, but they focus on the most dramatic ones. And to keep the audience interested you have to have something exciting going on all the time. In real life most people don't have as many things happen in their lives as the characters do in a soap.

Also, relationships don't break down quite so often in real life. That's because in a soap the cast keeps changing. For example, when an actor or actress decides to leave, this character is written out of the script and a new one is introduced.

In groups

Discuss what you learn from these statements about how far the characters and stories in soaps are true to life and why they are different from real life.

What the actress says:

My job is to make my character seem real, but she's not! I'm just playing a part.

It's nice to be recognised when I'm walking down the street. But it worries me a bit when people call after me using my character's name. Some of them seem to think I'm really her.

In fact, I'm a very different sort of person to her. I don't speak like her. I'm just putting on an accent. And I certainly don't think like her. In real life I'd never dream of doing most of the things I have to pretend to do when I'm being her.

For your file

Write a review of a soap that you watch. What are the storylines? What are the dramatic events that the writer and director have included in order to capture your attention? How realistic are they? Have any new characters suddenly appeared in the script? Can you explain why they have appeared?

Every picture tells a story

It's often said that every picture tells a story. But the story it tells can be different, depending on:

- who is looking at the picture
- what viewpoint they have
- what message they want the picture to give.

For example, when a picture is shown on a television news bulletin, the way you look at it will be influenced by what the presenter or reporter says about it.

This picture (right) shows a British soldier on patrol in an Iraqi city after the war against Saddam Hussein.

A British soldier on patrol in Helmand Province helping the Afghan government to keep control after the war, in which helped drive out the Taliban.

A soldier from the occupying army, which invaded Afghanis and which continues to remain in the country illegally.

Just another example of the rain forest disappearing at an alarming speed, as it is cut down to make way for a road, without a thought for all the species that are being destroyed.

The new road is just one example of how the country's economic problems are being tackled by the government. It will provide a much-needed link along which minerals from the interior can be transported to the coast for export to Europe and the USA.

This picture (left) shows part of the tropical rainforest being cut down in order to build a new road. Above and below the photo are two alternative news commentaries, presenting the construction of the road from different viewpoints.

For your file

Find a picture from a magazine or newspaper and write two alternative commentaries for it that present it from different points of view.

Viewpoint matters

The use of different camera angles can also affect how you 'read' what you see on film, or even in a still photo. If you watch a TV news story about a conflict – for instance, between the police and a group of demonstrators – it makes a big difference whether the film is shot from behind the police, or from behind the demonstrators.

It's easy to see only one side of the story.

The hero's **point of view**

When you watch a TV drama or a film, you often get to see the action from a particular point of view: that of the hero or heroine. The story is told from their perspective and the camera looks at events through their eyes. Their thoughts and feelings, and their beliefs and needs, are what move the story forward.

For instance, think of a serious TV drama like *The Bill* – the point of view is always that of the police and never that of the criminals they are chasing. Then contrast with the classic comedy *Only Fools and Horses*, where the perspective is still from the hero's point of view – but this time the hero is a petty criminal.

In both cases we end up liking the main characters – whether they're 'good' or 'bad' – because they're the characters we're told most about and the characters we're given the most to identify with. We don't generally stop to try to see things from the other characters' points of view.

Even news items are often presented from only one point of view. We tend to think the news is unbiased – or that it should be. But the news often presents only one aspect of a story, or allows one aspect of a story to dominate.

The voice-over that accompanies film of an event might 'tell us what to think' about what we see. The people interviewed might be asked only particular questions, or the film might be edited to include only one sort of answer.

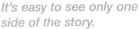
In groups

1 Discuss what you learn about viewpoints in TV programmes from the extract (left). Then talk about the TV dramas and situation comedies you watch, and discuss whose point of view they are presented from.

2 Watch a recording of a TV news broadcast. Discuss the stories that were presented. Did they always present the whole story or did some of the items only focus on one aspect of the story? Do you think any of the stories were biased because they presented the story from only one viewpoint?

How do you handle your money?

Are you a spender or a saver? How good are you at handling your money? On your own, do this quiz to find out how well you look after your money. Keep a record of your answers and then check what your answers tell you about your money-management skills.

1 At the end of the week do you find yourself:

a Always out of pocket?

b Sometimes in credit, sometimes in debt?

c Usually with a little bit to spare?

2 When you get your pocket money do you:

a Usually spend it as soon as you get it?

b Roughly plan how you will spend it and hope it will last the week?

c Plan your budget carefully and keep a record of what you spend?

3 You get a windfall gift of £50 from a rich aunt. Do you:

a Splash out on those new DVDs you want?

b Spend half on DVDs and save the rest?

c Put it all into your savings account?

4 You want a new bicycle. Do you:

a Ask for one as a Christmas or birthday present?

b Discuss how much your parents are willing to contribute, and start saving the rest yourself?

c Set about raising the cash yourself?

5 You hear that the newsagent wants someone to do an early morning paper round. Do you:

a Say you're not interested, because you don't like getting up early?

b Say you'll take the job?

c Go and ask about the pay and conditions, then decide whether or not to apply?

6 Your brother's birthday is coming up. Do you:

a Hope your parents will give you enough to buy him a decent present?

b Frantically start doing without things to save up enough to buy him a present of some sort?

c Draw out the money you've earmarked for his present from your savings account?

7 You're going away on the family summer holiday in a few weeks and will need some spending money. Do you:

a Trust to luck that your parents will give you some?

b Hope you'll be able to save a few pounds from what you already get each week?

c See if you can find some extra jobs to get you some extra money?

8 You want a new pair of expensive trainers, but your parents say you can only have a less expensive pair. Do you:

a Pester your parents until they fork out the money?

b Ask your gran to lend you some money to make up the difference, and arrange to pay her back when you can?

c Save something each week till you've enough to pay the difference?

9 You want to buy a new MP3 player. Do you:

a Go into the nearest shop and buy the first one you see?

b Get one like your friend's because she seemed to pay a reasonable price?

c Check out the prices yourself and see where you can get the best deal?

10 A friend is desperate for cash to buy a new jumper she wants. Do you:

a Offer to lend her some money from your savings?

b Tell her it's her problem and you can't help?

c Discuss ways of helping her to raise the money?

What your answers say about how you handle your money

Mostly 'a's

It probably seems as though you never have any money! That's because, quite frankly, you're not very good at handling it. You need to think more carefully before you spend your money, and start taking more responsibility for how you spend it by planning a budget. Also, you tend to rely on your parents to give you money when you need it, rather than either saving it up or earning some extra money for yourself.

Mostly 'b's

You are beginning to understand how to handle money. You make some sensible decisions, but sometimes you may find yourself short of cash when you needn't be. You need to make sure you always think ahead and put enough by, so that you don't have to depend on others when you want to buy presents or have cash to spend on your holidays.

Mostly 'c's

You're careful with your money and already good at managing it. You realise that you need to plan ahead by saving up for things, and when you haven't got enough for what you want, you are prepared to do something about trying to raise the money yourself. But make sure you keep a balanced attitude towards your money and don't just hoard it!

In pairs

Discuss what your answers told you about your money-management skills. Are you a spender or a saver? Tell each other what you think each of you needs to do to improve your money-management skills. Each write down two things you have learned from the quiz about how you manage your money.

Money-management tips

Many people find themselves short of money long before the end of the week. Usually it's because they don't plan their spending carefully enough.

Here are some tips for you:

1. Put half of your pocket money into a money box, and don't take it out until half way through the week. Or get your parents to give you pocket money in instalments.

2. Avoid impulse buys. Don't be tempted to spend your money on something you haven't planned to spend it on, just because you are wandering around a shop and happen to see something that looks nice.

3. Learn to plan a budget (see page 55).

Pocket money matters

Most children are given pocket money each week by their parents. But there is no law saying that your parents must do this. Some parents simply cannot afford to give their children pocket money on a regular basis.

> "Whatever your folks give you, big or small, it is never enough. It is, though, probably all they can afford."
>
> **Ros Asquith**

What should your pocket money be for?

In groups

1 Divide a piece of paper into two columns. In one column, list the things you think you should have to use your pocket money to pay for, such as sweets and CDs. In the other column, list the things you think your parents should pay for, such as clothes and school trips.

Add to the lists any other items you can think of, either that your parents should pay for or that you think should be paid out of your pocket money.

Then compare your lists and share your ideas in a class discussion

2 Discuss the idea of having a pocket money contract, in which you agree with your parent(s) or guardian how much you have, what things the money is to be used for and what you agree to do in return for getting pocket money.

Pocket money problems

"My parents give me an allowance and expect me to buy all my own things. I have to buy all the things I need for school and all my own clothes. I have to buy my own soap and shampoo, and they expect me to budget so that I'll have enough money left over to buy presents. I know they are trying to get me to manage money myself, but the trouble is they don't give me enough. And they get very cross when I keep asking them for extra money so that I can go out with my friends. What can I do?"

Tom

"My problem is that my parents won't give me any pocket money unless I do chores. They say that pocket money's got to be earned. When I tell them my friends are given pocket money without having to earn it, they say that they're doing it for my own good to teach me the value of money. I don't think it's fair."

Javed

"I'm fed up. It's been weeks since I've had any pocket money, because my parents keep on stopping it for one reason or another. If I get into trouble at school, my parents stop my pocket money. If I get into trouble at home, they stop my pocket money. It's getting me down. I've even been tempted to take money from my mum's purse."

Ailsa

In pairs

Discuss Tom's problem. What do you think of the idea of being given an allowance rather than pocket money, and being expected to pay for everything yourself except your food and accommodation?

Discuss Javed's problem. Do you think pocket money should be a reward? Or should you expect to be given pocket money with no strings attached?

Discuss Ailsa's problem. Should you only get your pocket money if you are well behaved? Is stopping your pocket money a fair way of punishing you for doing something wrong?

For your file

Draft a letter of advice to either Tom, Javed or Ailsa.

What do you do with your pocket money?

In groups

Discuss what you do with your pocket money.

1 Do you spend it mainly on consumable items, such as sweets, snacks and soft drinks, comics and magazines, and make-up?

2 Do you spend it on your hobbies, or on CDs, DVDs and computer games?

3 Do you spend it on entertainments – going to the cinema or discos or to watch sporting events?

4 Do you save some of it, either to buy yourself something big, such as a guitar, or so that you can buy people presents at birthdays or festivals such as Christmas and Diwali?

5 Do you plan carefully how you are going to spend or save it by working out a budget, or do you just spend and then wait for the next week's handout?

Talk about things that affect the way you spend your money. Would you say you are:
a) careful with your money; **b)** quite careful; **c)** not very careful? Explain why.

Planning a budget

1 Estimate what your income is going to be over the next four weeks – the total amount of money you will get from pocket money, handouts and any cash you earn from doing odd jobs.

2 Write down exactly how you plan to use that money. Start by deciding whether or not you want to save any of the money. Write down the amount you want to save and deduct that sum from the total amount.

3 List the various items you are going to spend money on and how much you plan to spend on each item. It may be helpful to divide the items into essentials (E) and non-essentials (NE).

4 Add up the cost of everything you want to spend your money on. If it is more than your total income, you will have to cross out some of the items until the cost equals the amount you have to spend.

5 Keep a record of how much you spend each week, so that you can check that you are keeping to your budget.

'I've spent my school trip money'

Role play

There are only four weeks to go to the school trip to France. Your best friend suddenly announces they won't be coming. When you ask them why, they explain that instead of paying in the money their parents have been sending in for the trip, they've been spending it on themselves. They know they are going to be in terrible trouble when their parents find out. What do you think they should do?

In pairs, role play the scene in which your friend tells you what they've done and together you discuss what they should do now.

For your file

Work out a budget plan for the next four weeks. The flow-chart on the left shows you how.

You and your parents

Until you are 18-years-old, you are considered too young to make all your own decisions. The adult, or adults, who are in charge of you must look after you and make some decisions for you.

If you live with both your parents, they usually share this responsibility. But if they split up, a court may have to decide who is to be responsible for you.

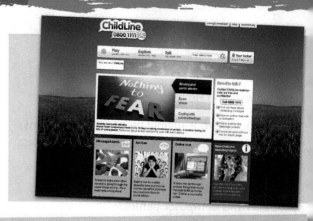

Your rights at home

■ When can I leave home?

It's your parents' duty to care and look after you until you are 18. That's the age at which the law says you can leave home without your parents' permission. However, parents can't usually make you stay if you are over 16 and don't want to do so.

■ Must they give me pocket money?

No. There is no law which says that parents must give children pocket money.

■ Can my parents hit me?

Your parents have the right and duty to discipline you and can decide how to punish you. This may include smacking you. But any physical punishment must not be too harsh. Parents are not allowed to hit you too hard and beat you up. That is physical abuse for which parents can be prosecuted and their children taken into care.

■ Can my parents make me go to the school they choose?

Yes. They have the right to choose which school you go to. But there is no guarantee that they will get the school of their choice.

■ Can they choose my religion for me?

Your parents can decide the religion in which you are brought up. If they disagree, because they have different beliefs, they can ask a court to decide. The judge will decide what is in your best interests. Depending on your age, your own views will be taken into consideration and, as long as it is clear that you understand what is involved, you will probably be allowed to make up your own mind.

■ If I need medical treatment, who makes the decisions?

When you are 16 you can choose your own doctor and give permission yourself for any surgical, medical or dental treatment you need. When they are treating someone under the age of 16, doctors are advised – where possible –

to obtain permission from parents, unless it is an emergency or the young person is clearly able to understand what the treatment involves.

■ If my parents split up, can I choose who I want to live with?

If your parents disagree, a court will decide who you go to live with. But what you want to do is very important and you will be asked where you want to go.

■ If my dad doesn't live with us can my mum stop me seeing him?

You have the right to go on seeing your dad, if you want to do so. If your parents cannot agree about it, a court will have to decide what is best for you.

■ What if I'm adopted?

If you are adopted, it means you get new parents – because your natural parents have died or cannot look after you for some reason. Your new parents take over all the duties and responsibilities from your natural parents.

At 18, adopted people have the right to see a copy of their original birth records and can contact the agency that arranged the adoption to ask for more information about their birth relatives.

ChildLine is the UK's free, confidential 24 hour helpline and online service dedicated to children and young people provided by the NSPCC.

The Helpline is on 0800 1111 or you can find out more and contact them through their website: www.childline.org.uk

Parents' duties and children's rights

Children have the right to be looked after properly by their parents. It is the duty of parents to care for their children. They must make sure that you are properly fed and clothed. When you are ill, they must see that you get proper medical treatment. It is their duty to send you to school, so that you get a proper education.

If your parents neglect you or treat you cruelly, they can be taken to court. The court has the power to take you away from your parents and order someone else to have custody of you. It can order you to be taken into care by the local authority. You may be placed in a children's home or sent to live with foster parents.

In pairs

Study the information on these pages. Decide which of the statements below are TRUE and which are FALSE.

1 You can leave home without your parents' permission when you are 16.

2 Your parents have no legal duty to pay you pocket money.

3 Your parents have the right to smack you as hard and as often as they like.

4 Parents must take children's views into consideration when choosing a school for them.

5 Your parents can choose which religion you are brought up in.

6 Once you are 14 you can make your own decisions about any medical treatment you need.

7 If your parents split up, you have the right to choose who you live with.

8 If you live apart from your dad, your mum can stop you seeing him.

9 Foster parents have all the same rights and responsibilities as natural parents.

10 Adopted children aged 14 and over have the right to see their birth records.

In groups

Discuss the statements below and say why you agree or disagree with them. Choose someone to note down your different ideas and share your views in a class discussion.

"Parents should ask children which school they'd like to go to, but it's right that parents should make the final decision, not children."

"Smacking is a good way of disciplining children and doesn't do any harm. It would be ridiculous to make it illegal, as it is in several other European countries."

"Young people over the age of 13 should be able to make their own decisions about medical treatments without their parents having to be told."

Children and the law

Young children do not have the same rights as adults. There are a number of things you are not allowed to do until you reach a certain age. The law aims to protect you by not letting you do these things until you are old enough to do them in a responsible way.

The chart on the right shows some of these things.

In groups

Some people think that certain laws are out of date. They think that the ages at which young people can do things should be changed. What do you think?

Talk about the laws and list any changes you think should be made. Then share your ideas in a class discussion.

For your file

Write about the laws concerning the age at which you can do things. Say which ones you think are important because of the way they protect young people, and which ones (if any) you think are out of date and should be changed.

At Birth
An adult can open a savings account for you at a bank or a building society.

If your parents want, they can get you a passport.

At 5
You can buy or rent a U or PG category DVD.

You can drink alcohol in private.

At 7
You can open and draw money from a National Savings account or Trustee Savings Bank account.

At 10
You can be held responsible for any crime you commit.

Most banks or building societies will let you open an account.

At 12
You can buy a pet.

You can rent or buy a category 12 DVD.

At 13
You can have a part-time job, provided that it does not interfere with your schoolwork, and you do not work more than a certain number of hours each day.

At 14
You can go into a bar on your own, but you cannot buy or drink alcohol there.

At 15
You can rent or buy a category 15 DVD.

At 16
You can leave school and work full-time.

You can drink beer, cider or wine with a meal in a pub or hotel.

You can drive a moped.

You can get married with your parents' permission.

You can choose your own doctor and give permission yourself for any surgical, medical or dental treatment you need.

You can join the armed forces with parental consent.

At 17
You can drive a car or motorbike.

At 18
You can get married without parental consent.

You can vote in general and local elections.

You can own land, buy a house or flat, hold a tenancy and apply for a mortgage.

You can buy and drink alcohol in a bar.

You can join the armed forces without your parents' consent.

You can buy or rent a category 18 DVD.

You can buy cigarettes and tobacco.

Children in care

Around 89,000 children in the UK are being looked after in care. This means that a court has decided that it is in the best interests of the child for the local authority to take over the responsibility for their care.

Why are you taken into care?

There are many different reasons why a person may be taken into care. Here are some of the main reasons:

- Your parents have died or abandoned you and there is no adult to look after you.
- Your parents neglect you or treat you cruelly.
- You repeatedly play truant and no one can get you to go to school.
- You are convicted of having committed a serious criminal offence.
- Your parents are unable to look after you because they are ill or homeless.
- A court decides that you are in 'moral danger', for example of being abused.

How long do you stay in care?

It depends on why you are put into care. Some children stay for only a few weeks. Others may stay until they are 18.

Where do you live when you are in care?

It depends on what the court decides and what is available at the time. A social worker will make recommendations on where you should live, which school you should go to and how often you should see your family. Some children in care are allowed to live at home. Others live in foster homes or in community homes.

Can you ask to go into care?

If the situation is very bad at home, for example, if you are being physically or sexually abused, or not being properly fed and cared for, you can contact the social services department and ask to see a social worker. They will give you advice on what can be done to help you.

If you do not like being in care is there anything you can do about it?

When a court decides to take you into care, it makes a care order. Depending on the circumstances, a care order can last until you are 18. But you can appeal against the order at once or apply to have it ended at any time. The Children's Legal Centre can give you advice if you want to try to have your care order ended.

"I had to live with a foster family for a while because my mum was seriously ill and there was no one who could look after me while she was in hospital. I was miserable at first, but my foster parents were really kind and understanding. I still see them sometimes."

Sonia

"At first I missed being at home, but then I realised that it wasn't my fault and I was better off where I was. My key worker has helped me a lot and I've made friends with another girl who's had the same kind of problems I've had."

Leanne

"I was worried that everyone at school would treat me differently, because I'd been taken into care. But it hasn't made any difference."

Darren

In groups

Study the information on this page, then discuss these questions.

1 What is a care order?

2 Why are children taken into care?

3 How long do care orders last?

4 Where do children in care live?

5 What do you learn from the comments about how children feel about being in care?

The rights of the child

The United Nations Convention on the Rights of the Child was agreed on 20 November 1989. It has now been accepted and ratified by all but two governments in the world (the USA and Somalia).

The convention consists of 54 rights that every child has. Here are some of the most important ones.

1 The right to have a name from birth and to be granted a nationality.

2 The right to express opinions and have those opinions considered in matters which affect their well-being.

3 The right to freedom of thought, conscience and religion subject to parental guidance and national law.

4 Protection from all forms of physical or mental violence, neglect or maltreatment.

5 Protection from employment that is likely to harm or to interfere with their development and education, especially drug trafficking and sexual exploitation.

6 The right to the highest standards of health and health care facilities.

7 The right to free education at primary level.

8 The right to special protection for children who are refugees, disabled, orphans or of minority ethnic groups.

In groups

1 Study the list of some of the main rights of the child. Then discuss what other rights you think children have.

Think about:

- Survival rights – the right to the basic necessities for a healthy life.

- Development rights – the right to learn and have access to play, leisure and cultural activities and to develop their own views and ideas.

- Protection rights – the right to be protected from cruelty, abuse and exploitation.

- Participation rights – the right to have a say in matters that affect their lives.

2 Draw up a charter of children's rights. Here's the beginning of 'A Children's Charter' drawn up by a Year 7 class at Attleborough High School, Norfolk:

> 1 All children have the right to be loved.

Child employment in Britain

Child employment in Britain is governed by the 1933 Children and Young Persons Act. Its main provisions are:

- Children under 13 are prohibited from working.

- Children under 16 years old:
  - must not work during the school day
  - must not work before 7.00 am and after 7.00 pm
  - must not work for more than two hours on a school day or a Sunday
  - must not carry, lift or move objects so heavy as to be likely to cause injury.

In groups

Study the laws governing child employment in Britain (above).

Discuss the reasons for each of the main rules. Do you think the laws should be changed in any way? Make notes of your views, then share them in a class discussion.

Child labour in the developing world

The International Labour Organisation estimated in 2006 that there were about 168 million child workers in the world.

There are five main types of jobs done by children in developing countries:

- Domestic work, including cooking
- Non-paid work, which takes place mainly on farms
- Tied or bonded labour, to pay off the debts their parents or grandparents have built up
- Wage labour, which might be regular or casual
- Marginal activities, which often take place on the streets, for example, 'looking after' cars

"I was made to work in a carpet factory where I lived in Lahore, because my parents had borrowed money from the carpet manufacturer to pay for my brother's wedding. I was twelve years old. Luckily I could go home after each 14-hour day: the other children worked till midnight and slept among the looms.**"**

Iqbal, from Lahore, Pakistan

"My mother was sick all the time. We had no food for me, my sister and brothers. I started to wash the car windscreens at the traffic lights. I was nine. Now I sell sweets, chewing gum and pulseras (friendship bracelets) outside the bus station. The bus drivers let me on their big buses. I earn good money and take it to my mother. She doesn't hit me any more because I bring her the money.**"**

A 10-year-old street vendor, Guadeloupe

Sawai's story

Sawai Langlah, of Srisaket province in north-east Thailand, had to find work at the age of 13 when her father suddenly became paralysed. She had to leave school and get a job far from home in the capital, Bangkok, through a cousin who was already working in a small garment factory. She decides to find out for herself (right).

For your file

Read Sawai's story and the statements of the other two child workers (above). Either write a short statement explaining your reactions to the stories – what you think and feel about the children and their lives, or imagine you are a child labourer who spends all day working for hardly any pay in a garment or carpet factory, with breaks only to eat and sleep, and write a letter or diary entry describing your thoughts and feelings.

Because I knew nothing about sewing I had to learn everything from scratch. My employer said I would have to do domestic work to repay him for the training I would receive.

It was a very small family business – a three-storey house that was also the owner's home. I was paid very little – 500 baht ($25) a month. Out of that I had to pay back 100 baht for my housing and my food; although they gave us only cooked rice, and if we wanted anything with it then we had to buy it.

There were six people working in the factory and we all shared one room. The room we worked in was very narrow with about five machines in it and the lighting was very poor. I worked from eight in the morning to midnight. This was a privilege. My cousin often stayed up sewing until two in the morning.

I was supposed to be an apprentice but I wasn't really given any training. I had to do a lot of housework. I washed clothes and cleaned the house and kitchen. I could be called to do it at any time. I was lucky to have my cousin there; when my employer was out she would teach me and I would also watch how the others worked. That's how I got trained.

Developing a product

In order to develop a product, there are several different stages that you need to go through. These are: deciding on an idea, doing some market research, designing your product, testing your product and then doing a market presentation.

Many jobs involve working as part of a team. The group activity on these pages involves working as a team to develop and design a product for a competition.

Invent a new game

A competition for a game for 9–13 year olds, designed by 9–13 year olds.

Games Workplace is offering you the chance to join the ranks of the country's top game designers.

Rules:

1 All of the different stages of developing your game must be carried out by people aged 9–13. There should be four or five of you in each group.

2 The game must be a board or card game suitable for 9–13 year olds.

3 To enter the competition, you must develop and design a sample product of the game. This should include either the board and pieces, or a set of cards.

4 You should also include a clear set of rules. These should be written as an instruction leaflet, showing how the game is played, with examples.

Play testing of the game by 9–13 year olds will be encouraged, to make your game as good as possible. Any changes made as a result of play testing will be encouraged, and awarded extra marks by the judges.

In groups

Prepare an entry for this competition. Follow the advice given on these pages and develop and design your product in stages.

Stage 1 Deciding on an idea

Study the competition rules and hold a brainstorming session in which you share ideas. Talk about different types of board and card games. Which do you enjoy most? What sort of game might you develop?

Appoint someone to act as secretary and write down the ideas you suggest on a large sheet of paper.

Stage 2 Market research

Market research is one of the most important stages in developing your product. You can design a game that looks really good, but if nobody likes it, it won't sell.

The word 'market' refers to anyone who will buy your game. The more you know about your market, the more chance you have of developing a game that will appeal to it.

Research the market for your game by:

● Studying other games. Look at games that you, your family and your friends have – which ones do they like and why?

● Walking around a toy or games shop to see what different types of games they have. Talk to the shop owner. Ask them which games are most popular and why.

● Carrying out a survey to find out which games are most popular in the 9–13 age group. To do this you will need to design a market research questionnaire. Think carefully about what questions you will ask.

● Looking on the Internet at different games and discussing which are popular and why.

Stage 3 Designing your product

Follow the steps in the flowchart (right) to design your game.

Stage 4 Market testing or piloting

Get another group to test the game by playing it. Watch what happens when they play the game. What were the best bits? What were the worst? Does the game need changing in any way to make it better?

Give your test group a questionnaire, and ask for comments on the game. Some of the questions could be as follows:

> What do you think the good points of the game are? Why?
> _____
>
> What do you think the bad points of the game are? Why?
> _____
>
> Did you find the instructions easy or difficult to follow? Why?
> _____
>
> Did you enjoy playing the game? Why?
> _____
>
> How do you think the game could be improved?
> _____
>
> Do you think it is more or less enjoyable than other similar games?
> _____

Make any changes to your game as a result of your market testing.

Stage 5 Market presentation

Choose a member of your group to act as a spokesperson. Get them to demonstrate your game to the rest of the class. They should explain what the game is and how you developed it, and then answer any questions the class might have.

For your file

Write a promotion flyer (advert) for your game, explaining how you play it and why people should buy it.

Discuss what you have found out in your market research.

▼

Look again at the ideas suggested in your brainstorming session.

▼

Add any new ideas that you may have thought of as a result of your market research.

▼

Decide which game you are going to develop.

▼

Discuss the details of the game. For example, What do you need to do to win? How do you play? What are the rules?

▼

Using paper and card, produce a sample copy of the game and sample instructions and rules.

Selling your product – taking a risk

Imagine that the judges of the competition liked your group's idea. They have offered you a loan of £100 towards the cost of producing some copies of the game to sell at future school events. The loan is made on condition that you must pay it back within a year. However, if you make more than £100 from the sale of the game, you will be able to pay back the loan and keep the extra money yourselves as profit.

The cost of production

Before you decide whether to accept the loan, you need to work out the cost of producing the game, how much you can sell it for and whether or not you can make a profit.

First of all you need to think about the materials and packaging:

- **Materials** The more expensive materials you use, the higher your production costs will be. But more expensive materials usually produce a higher quality product.
- **Packaging** Board games and card games are usually packaged in eye-catching boxes. This makes customers want to buy them. The inside of the box needs to be divided up. This is to keep the pieces safe. The pieces or cards need to be easily taken in or out of the box.

In groups

When you are deciding which materials to choose to use for making your game, you need to remember that it is important to make your game look good. Discuss how you could do this.

Does the game have cards? Pieces? A board? What should they look like?

In groups

- Read the case study. Discuss what materials you would need to manufacture copies of your game. Find out the cost of the materials and work out how much it would cost to make **a)** 10 **b)** 20 **c)** 50 copies of your game.
- Discuss what price you would need to charge for your game in order to make enough money to be able to pay back a loan of £100.
- Decide whether you would be willing to take the risk of borrowing £100 for a year in order to make and sell your game.
- If you plan to go ahead, you need to decide who is going to do the manufacturing. Which members of the team will be responsible for this? Decide who will do what.

Case study
Setting the price

Jack's group found that the cost of materials per copy varied from £4 to £6 depending on the quality. They decided to use materials costing £5 per copy.

Setting a price for your product is very important. If you set a low price, you may sell more copies of your game, but you won't make as much profit. If Jack's group priced the game at £6, they would only make £1 profit per game sold (£6 income minus £5 for materials). That means they would have to sell 100 copies of the game in order to pay back the loan of £100.

If you set too high a price, fewer people are likely to buy the game. If Jack's group priced the game at £15, they would make a profit of £10 per game sold. That means that they would only have to sell ten copies of the game in order to pay back the loan. But would they sell ten copies at that price?

So Jack's group decided to set the price of the game at £10. That meant that they would make a profit of £5 per game sold. They would have to sell 20 copies in order to pay back the loan. They thought that was possible.

Advertising your product

When a company launches a new product, they will advertise it. A series of different type of advertisements is an advertising campaign. The advertising campaign will have two main purposes:

1 To let likely customers know what the new product is and where they can buy it.

2 To inform customers of the product's special features.

Sometimes a product will have some features that are special only to it. These are known as their 'unique selling points' (or USPs).

The company will then decide the message of the advertising campaign.

If it's a car, it might be described as green, fast, spacious or stylish – or all four. It depends on the product. The campaign will focus on the USPs of the product, because these are what makes it special.

The company then has to decide where the advertising will take place, or the medium for the advertising. Big companies usually advertise in the following ways:

- TV
- Radio
- Newspapers
- Magazines
- Large posters
- The internet

Imagine you have to advertise your new game for sale at the next school social event. What advertising strategy will you have? Think about the following ideas:

- An advert on the school's website.
- A press release to your local radio station for some free publicity.
- Posters to go up around the school and in local shops.
- A leaflet to be delivered to all members of the school, or in the local area or made available in local shops.

For your file

Study a leaflet or a catalogue advertising toys. Look at the advertisements for board games. Which are the most effective? Say why you like them and why you think they work.

Drugs and how they affect you

What do we mean by 'drugs'?

A drug is a substance that alters the way your mind or body works. There are thousands of different drugs. Some of them are natural products, found in plants and trees. Others are synthetic products, which are manufactured by chemical processes.

Drugs can be divided into three categories – medicinal drugs, social drugs and illegal drugs.

Social drugs. These are drugs in everyday use, which are not banned by law. The most common is caffeine, a mild stimulant which is found in coffee, tea, chocolate and some soft drinks. The two other socially acceptable drugs are alcohol, found in drinks such as beers, wines and spirits, and nicotine which is found in tobacco.

While alcohol and nicotine are not banned, they are dangerous drugs. Excessive use of alcohol can lead to alcoholism and death from cirrhosis of the liver. The nicotine in tobacco can lead to addiction to cigarette smoking, which can cause heart conditions and lung cancer.

Medicinal drugs. These are drugs you can take if your doctor prescribes them. They can be used to cure infections, to control diseases, such as asthma, or to relieve painful conditions, such as arthritis.

Medicinal drugs also include certain drugs that are considered safe for you to use without consulting your doctor, such as aspirin and cough mixture. You can buy these drugs from chemist's shops or supermarkets.

Illegal drugs. These are drugs that it is against the law for you either to possess or to sell, because they are considered to be so dangerous and harmful. They include heroin, cocaine, LSD, ecstasy and cannabis. When people use the terms 'drugs' and 'drugtaking', they are usually referring to the use of illegal drugs.

Some people divide illegal drugs into 'hard drugs' and 'soft drugs'. 'Hard drugs' are very powerful and dangerous drugs such as heroin and cocaine. They are addictive and physically harmful, and can lead to severe withdrawal symptoms when someone tries to give them up. 'Soft drugs', such as cannabis, do not cause withdrawal symptoms when someone stops using them, but may have long-term effects and are psychologically addictive.

What is drug abuse?

Drug abuse is when any drug, such as heroin, is used for a purpose for which it is not intended, or when it has not been prescribed for medical reasons.

From *Drugs* by Anita Naik

There is no proper definition of drug abuse or misuse. Often it is simply a judgement made by society about what is a bad or wrong use of drugs. What one person thinks is drug abuse another person may not. What is drug abuse – ten cups of coffee a day, five pints of lager at lunchtime or one cannabis cigarette?

In groups

Study the two definitions of drug abuse. Decide your group's definition of drug abuse and compare it with other people's definitions in a class discussion.

Talk about how society regards some drugs as acceptable, while making other drugs illegal.

In pairs

'If alcohol and tobacco had only been discovered recently, they would be banned. The reason why they aren't banned is because their use is so widespread that everyone accepts it. Really, they are just as harmful as the drugs that are illegal.' Discuss this view.

Why is there so much concern about drugtaking?

If you take drugs, it can affect your life in many different ways. It depends, of course, on which drugs you use and how often you take them. The article below describes the different ways in which drugs can affect you.

How drugs can affect you

Health Your health may be damaged. If you take drugs regularly, your body may get so used to a particular drug that it develops a tolerance to the drug. You keep on having to take more and more of it to get the same effect. You may find that your body becomes so dependent on the drug that you cannot stop taking it without suffering from withdrawal symptoms. You are then addicted to the drug, so that you cannot stop taking it even if you want to.

Regular drugtakers often get physical illnesses too. They may lose weight, get sores on their bodies and pick up infections easily. If they inject drugs and share needles, they run the risk of catching hepatitis or HIV and then developing AIDS.

Relationships Your relationships with your family and friends may be affected. Drugtakers often try to conceal their habit from their families. They may become moody and depressed. Drugtaking can take over their lives to such an extent that they lose interest in the things they used to do with their friends and spend all their time with other drugtakers.

Work Your work may suffer. Drugtakers can find it hard to concentrate and may start to fall behind in their schoolwork. If they have a job, they may get sacked for not working properly.

Crime You may get into trouble with the police. Because you are taking an illegal substance, you may find yourself arrested for possession and taken to court. When a person is addicted to a drug, they need extra money to pay for the larger amounts of the drug that they need in order to satisfy their craving for it. Drug addicts often turn to crime in order to obtain the money to feed their habit. They may get involved in shoplifting or stealing money from their relatives and friends.

Drugs can kill

Most young people who take drugs will not kill themselves. But taking too many drugs at any one time is very dangerous. The more drugs a person takes, the more chance there is that they will have an accident, such as choking on their own vomit while they are unconscious.

It is also very dangerous to mix drugs. Much smaller amounts of drugs can be fatal when they are taken together than if they are taken separately.

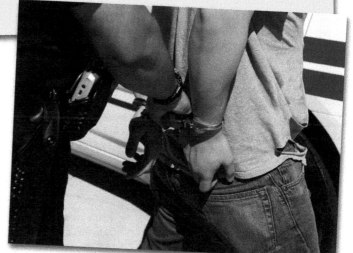

In groups

Discuss the various ways that drugtaking can affect a person's life. Each write down how dangerous you think drugtaking is: **a)** extremely dangerous; **b)** quite dangerous; **c)** not very dangerous; **d)** safe. Compare your results. Do you think adults are too concerned about drugtaking?

In pairs

Use the information on this page to help you to produce a glossary of terms people use when discussing drugs and drugtaking: addiction, dependence, drug abuse, hard drugs, soft drugs, tolerance, withdrawal symptoms.

For your file

Design a poster to warn people your age about the dangers of drugtaking. You could use the library or resources centre to find out further information about drugs and drugtaking and then include it in your poster.

Young people and drugs

Why do people start taking drugs?

If you listen to what the papers say, you may think that young people take drugs because they're forced into it by evil dealers or because they're bored and fed up and can't think of anything better to do. While some people may drink or take drugs out of boredom, the fact is that all kinds of people have all kinds of reasons.

- Some do it because the thought of missing out on an 'amazing' experience is just too much for them.
- Others try it because they feel bad about themselves and hope a drug will make them feel better.
- Some people just do it to escape from their lives, others to fit in with their friends.

There isn't any one reason why people take drugs.

I take drugs because my friends do. I wanted to show them I was one of them. I was afraid of being left out.

I'd heard such a lot about drugs and it sounded exciting. I was curious to find out what it felt like.

I suppose the real reason I'm into drugs is to escape from all the problems I've got at home.

If I'm honest, I got into drugtaking because I wanted to appear grown-up. I wanted to show off.

There's nothing to do around here and they're easy to get hold of, so I thought I'd give them a try.

I wanted to show everyone that they couldn't tell me what to do. That I was going to do what I wanted whatever they might say.

It gives you a thrill doesn't it? You're doing something that's illegal and that adults are always telling you that you shouldn't do.

I felt miserable and depressed. I started taking drugs to try to cheer myself up.

I take them for fun. I know it's risky, but who cares?

to show off
out of boredom
out of curiosity
for excitement
to feel grown-up
to keep in with friends
to escape from personal problems
as a way of rebelling

In groups

What do you think are the main reasons why young people start to experiment with drugs? Study the statements on this page and, on your own, list the reasons given on the left in order, starting with what you consider to be the main reason.

If you can suggest any other reasons, include them in your list.

Compare your views, then produce a group statement to share with the rest of the class.

What is your attitude to drugs and drugtaking?

Cannabis: the dangers

While cannabis is not physically addictive, about 10% of users become psychologically dependent on it.

Experts believe that smoking one joint causes the same damage to the lungs as smoking five cigarettes. So it increases the risk of you getting lung cancer and other lung problems.

Using cannabis can have long-term effects. Cannabis has been linked with mental health disorders, including schizophrenia and psychosis. Long term users may develop problems with their memory and their ability to concentrate, particularly if they start smoking at an early age.

Skunk is a type of herbal cannabis, which can be 2–3 times stronger than other types of cannabis and, therefore, is more dangerous.

Because it can be so harmful, the government reclassified cannabis from a Class C drug to a Class B drug in 2009.

'I'm really worried about my brother, because I've found out that he's started smoking cannabis. What should I do?' Fay, 12

Your brother may not realise that he's messing up – many young people who smoke cannabis are convinced that it is harmless, and genuinely don't see a problem.

In fact, cannabis isn't harmless. Regular use can make people unmotivated and it can lead people to experiment with other, more dangerous drugs. Cannabis can be expensive, getting people into debt or crime, and, like tobacco, smoking joints can cause serious lung damage. Perhaps most important of all, cannabis is an illegal drug – it can land users with a criminal record, and that would do nothing for your brother's future job prospects.

Do your brother a favour and get hold of the facts – call the National Drugs Helpline on 0800 776600, explain your dilemma and ask for more information. Let your brother know that you are worried for him. Don't judge him, but show him the facts behind your concern and let him think them through. Hopefully, he'll suss that drugs don't equal happiness.

FRANK, the national drugs helpline (0300 123 6600 and website (www.talktofrank.com), will give you all the facts you need to know about drugs.

People are pressurised into drugs

I think the thing with drugs is getting quite bad because there are so many people doing it. And the people that are dealing in it, they get into groups or gangs and pressurise people.

I think you can have your fun without taking drugs. Most people take them because they're pressurised. And there are people taking them in front of their mates to impress them, and when they're out – to have fun.

I think that they shouldn't take them because it can damage their health, and maybe they could die from them if they take too many. If they try once, I don't think they will suffer any damage. It's when they take them all the time, in clubs and things, that they end up in hospital.

My mum doesn't like anything to do with drugs. She tells me that if anyone pressurises me to take them, just to walk away, and not ever to take them, or I could end up in hospital and die.

Drugs don't frighten me. It's just not something I would have anything to do with.

Sammy, 13

In groups

Discuss what Sammy says in her statement, and say why you agree or disagree with her views. What is your attitude towards drugs and drugtaking?

Talk about Fay's problem and the advice that she is given. Imagine that you discovered your brother or sister was taking drugs. List the different actions you could take. Beside each action put the good and bad consequences of each action. Then decide what you would do and why.

For your file

Write a statement like Sammy's explaining why you think some people start to take drugs and what your views about drugs and drugtaking are.

Your neighbours and your neighbourhood

The way you behave affects other people – not just your family, but your neighbours, the people who live near you. While you have the right to expect your neighbours to behave towards you in a considerate way, it's your responsibility to behave considerately towards them.

What makes a good neighbour?

"I think a good neighbour is someone who keeps themselves to themselves and gets on with their life without bothering anyone else."

"A good neighbour is someone who isn't nosy and interfering, and doesn't complain about things like how loud you play your music."

"A good neighbour is someone you can rely on to help you out if you're in trouble."

"A good neighbour is someone you borrow things off and who doesn't mind if you can't pay them back."

"A good neighbour is someone who gets involved in the local community and tries to do things to improve the environment."

In groups

Discuss these comments. Say whether you agree or disagree with them and why. Then draft a statement saying what you think makes a good neighbour. Choose a spokesperson to read out your statement and share your views in a class discussion.

How to be a good neighbour

Hassan and Philip were asked to draw up a list of advice on how to be a good neighbour. Here's their list:

✗ Don't go on other people's property without permission.

✓ Always keep your pets under control. (If you have a dog, clear up its mess when you take it for a walk.)

✗ Don't play loud music where it will disturb other people.

✗ Don't ride your bicycle on the pavement.

✗ Don't drop litter.

✗ Don't spit or swear in public. Lots of people find it offensive.

✗ Don't vandalise property, even if it's derelict and due for demolition.

✓ Get involved in community action, such as schemes to tidy up the environment or improve leisure facilities in the neighbourhood.

✓ Offer to help people who find it hard to do things for themselves, such as older people or disabled people.

✓ Respect other people's privacy.

In pairs

Study Hassan and Philip's advice. Rank the pieces of advice they give in order of importance from 1 to 10, starting with 1 (the most important) and ending with 10 (the least important).

Are there any other important pieces of advice that you would have included on this list? If so, write them down, then join up with another pair and share your ideas in a group discussion.

Facilities and services

Has your neighbourhood got the right facilities for the different people who live there?

- Is there a good system of public transport to take people to the nearest town or shopping centre?

- Is there **a)** a shop; **b)** a post office; **c)** a surgery and health centre; **d)** a park or playground; **e)** a library; **f)** a swimming pool; **g)** a cinema within reach of most people's homes?

- Is there a community centre or village hall where people can meet and do various activities?

- Is there a youth centre?

In pairs

Discuss what facilities there are in your neighbourhood and decide what new facilities you would like to see provided. Then conduct a survey to find out what other people think about the facilities in your area. Try to get the views of different groups of people, from children to older people. Compare the views of the different groups and draft a report saying which facilities people would like to see provided or improved.

Safety

How safe is your neighbourhood?

- How safe are the roads? Are there any roads where the traffic travels so fast that they are dangerous? Are there safe places to cross? Are there cycle lanes so that it is safe for cyclists?

- How safe are the pavements? Are they in a good state of repair?

- Are the streets safe at night? Are they well-enough lit?

- Are the parks and playgrounds safe? Is any playground equipment in good condition? Are play areas fenced off?

- Are there any buildings that are dangerous because they are derelict?

In groups

Discuss how safe your neighbourhood is and suggest what needs to be done to make it safer. Appoint a spokesperson and share your ideas in a class discussion.

Appearance

How attractive is your neighbourhood?

- Is your neighbourhood clean and well cared for?

- Is there a lot of litter? Are there any places where people have dumped rubbish that needs clearing up?

- Are there flowerbeds and trees provided by the council? Are they in good condition or do they get vandalised?

- Is there a lot of graffiti?

- Is pollution a problem? Is the water in any local ponds, streams and rivers dirty or clean? What is the air quality like? Is the air polluted by traffic fumes?

In groups

Discuss how attractive the appearance of your neighbourhood is and suggest what could be done to improve its appearance. Appoint a spokesperson and share your ideas in a class discussion.

Vandalism – a costly problem

In many neighbourhoods, vandalism is a serious problem. Often it is public property that gets damaged. Repairing damage to public property costs local authorities thousands of pounds each year.

> "Vandals should have to pay for the damage they cause."

> "Vandals should have to repair any damage they do."

> "Vandals should have to spend their weekends doing community service."

> "They should be given a warning, then if they do it again they should be put away."

In groups

Study the pictures on this page. Discuss these questions, then share your views in a class discussion.

1 Can vandalism be dangerous as well as costly? Think of situations where this might be so.

2 Talk about why young people sometimes get involved in vandalism. Is boredom the main cause? What else causes vandalism – anger? frustration? jealousy? depression?

3 Imagine you saw someone carrying out an act of vandalism, what would you do? Would you report it to the owner of the property? Tell the police? Do nothing? Explain why.

4 If vandals are caught, how do you think they should be treated?

Role play

How would you feel if it was your property? In pairs, role play a scene in which an adult who has caught a young person committing an act of vandalism tells them off and explains why vandalising something is a serious matter.

In groups

How serious is writing graffiti? Does it depend where the graffiti is being written – on a toilet wall? on a bridge? on the wall of a public building, such as a library? on the wall of a private house?

For your file

Either write a story in which an act of vandalism leads to someone getting hurt, or design a poster which points out to young people how dangerous and costly vandalism is.

Taking action in the community

Street Scene champions

Many local councils have schemes in which members of the public can volunteer to be 'Local Environment' or 'Street Scene' champions. For example, Oxford City Council has such a scheme. As well as advising on recycling matters, 'Local Environment' champions encourage people to take a pride in their local area and join the campaign against enviro-crime such as flytipping, littering, graffiti, dog-fouling and flyposting.

In groups

What do you think of 'Local Environment' and 'Street Scene' champions? Are they a good idea? Or do you regard them as interfering busybodies who act as snoopers for the local council?

Would you consider becoming a 'Street Scene' champion when you are old enough? Would you join them if they asked for young volunteers to join in a clean-up campaign?

In groups

Think about your local environment. Is there anything that you think could be done either to make it a pleasanter place to live, or to improve the services and facilities available for the local community? For example:

- Is there any open space or park that could be developed to make it a nicer place to walk or play in?

- Is there somewhere, such as a stream or pond where people have dumped rubbish, that could be cleared and cleaned up?

- Are there any empty buildings, such as a hall or a cinema, that might be reopened or redeveloped in some way, for example, as a youth club?

Now follow the steps in the flow-chart (right).

Brainstorm ideas and appoint someone to act as spokesperson to share your ideas with the rest of the class.

⬇

Draw up a questionnaire and carry out a survey to find out what local people think of your ideas, and what other ideas they have for improving the area.

⬇

Analyse the results of the survey and discuss them together as a class.

⬇

Choose one of the ideas and draft an action plan, saying how you would put it into action and how you would finance it.

⬇

Invite a local councillor to come to the school to hear your proposal and discuss it with you. Ask them if there is any way you could go about raising the money to develop your project.

⬇

After their visit, discuss whether or not it is worth trying to take the project any further.

⬇

If you think it is, decide how you are going to do so.

What is a consumer?

A consumer is a person who buys goods and services for their own personal use.

We are all consumers. We all have certain needs, such as food, warmth and shelter, so the people who look after us buy us food to eat, clothes to wear and a home for us to live in.

We also buy things we want, rather than need. For example, we may buy a comic or a DVD. We may buy a ticket for the cinema or for a football match. We may buy a new T-shirt or a pair of trainers. What we buy will depend on what our personal interests are and what we can afford.

Services

As well as being consumers of goods, we are all consumers of services. Some of the services that we use we pay for directly. For example, if we go to the hairdressers, we pay the hairdresser to give us a haircut. If we go to a leisure centre for a swim, we pay to use the swimming pool.

At home, we need energy to provide power for heating and lighting, for cookers and washing machines, for televisions and computers. So we pay energy companies to supply us with the electricity, gas or oil that we use. We also need to have a supply of water for drinking and washing. So we pay a water company to supply us with clean water and also to get rid of our waste water.

Many of the other services that we need are provided by the government or by local councils. These include schools and colleges, the health service, refuse collection, the police service and the public library service. We pay for these services indirectly by taxes which are collected by the government and local councils.

In pairs

What is the difference between wanting things and needing things? Each draw up two lists – one of essential things (things you need) and one of things that you'd like to have (things you want).

Compare your lists with those of another pair. Does everyone have the same needs? Are your wants the same or different?

For your file

Write a short statement explaining what being a consumer means. Describe how we pay directly for some of the goods and services we buy, but indirectly for others.

Who influences what you buy?

There are many different factors that influence what you decide to buy.

Advertising You may have been made to feel that you will only be accepted if you are wearing a particular brand label or that you are missing out if you don't have a particular computer game.

Pressure from friends You might choose to buy something because all your friends have it. For example, they may all be wearing similar things and you don't want to look different or feel left out.

Fashion You may model your style on someone you've seen in a magazine or on a celebrity that you particularly admire.

Bargains You may see something in a shop that has had its price reduced or that seems to be being offered at a very good price.

Purchases that are made on the spur of the moment are called impulse purchases. If you make an impulse purchase or buy something because you are heavily influenced by other people, you are far more likely to feel disappointed with what you buy.

The golden rule is to think about what you really want to get before you go shopping. Know what you want to buy and if you can't find it, don't allow yourself to be tempted into buying something different.

To help yourself to avoid being disappointed, ask yourself these questions:

- What exactly am I looking for?
- Why do I want it?
- How often will I use it?
- How much can I afford to pay?
- Will it cost anything to look after?

Role play

Act out a scene in which a boy or girl, who has some birthday money to spend, goes shopping with a friend. They can't find what the person is looking for and the friend puts pressure on them to buy something that they don't really want. Take it in turns to be the person who is being pressurised and discuss which of you was the more successful at resisting the pressure.

In groups

Each think about advertising. How much is what you buy influenced by advertising – a lot? quite a lot? not much? Discuss the reasons for your answers.

For your file

Dear Erica

I've spent all my money on a jacket I didn't really want and couldn't really afford, just because my friend said I looked good in it and urged me to buy because it was on offer. How can I avoid making the same mistake again?

Imogen

Draft Erica's reply to Imogen.

Consumer rights and responsibilities

Being a good consumer means knowing what to look out for and what to avoid. It means knowing where and how to get the best value for money. And where to go if things go wrong. It means that as a consumer you have both rights and responsibilities.

What are my rights?

■ The right to choose

Consumer choice is something you might take for granted because you expect to be able to walk into a shop and take your pick from a selection of brands. Suppliers compete with one another to attract your attention and tempt you to buy their products and shop in their stores.

You might use a shop because it's near your home or because the prices are reasonable or because it always has what you want. You may often buy crisps, and always choose the same brand because you think they taste best and have more flavour. But you may choose a certain type of crisps because they have less fat than others. Or you may use a particular shampoo because you believe it makes your hair look shiny and feel soft.

But supposing you weren't given the option because there was only one company making crisps and one making shampoo. What if there was only one place that sold them? You'd have to take whatever they offered and pay whatever they asked or go without. You'd have no real choice.

■ The right to accurate information

Suppliers of goods and services should give out clear and accurate information so that you can compare them and choose what is best suited to your individual needs.

It is also important that you can rely on the information on labels, for example if you have a nut allergy, or whether the animal was free range.

■ The right to safety

You have the right to be sure that products are not going to put your life or health in danger. Manufacturers normally have to carry out rigorous safety tests and checks before they are allowed to put their goods into shops.

Some goods must be labelled with warnings or clear instructions for use. If you look at a bottle of disinfectant, or the label on an electric blanket, or the instructions for a new hairdryer, or a box of fireworks, you will see that they all have instructions to make sure that you use them safely.

Consumers, however, still have a responsibility to read and follow the instructions carefully. You can't blame the manufacturer or supplier if you choose to ignore the warnings.

■ The right to value for money

No one enjoys feeling that they've been cheated or conned into paying a high price for poor quality. But it can happen, unless you look carefully at what you're buying.

Remember that 'value' doesn't always mean 'cheapest'. Instead it means that the standard or

In groups

Talk about products that you buy regularly. Do you always buy the same brand? What influences your choice? Do you always use the same shops? Discuss why you choose to go to particular shops.

On your own, rank the five rights you have as a consumer in order of importance, then compare your lists. Discuss the reasons for any differences.

quality ought to be reflected in the price. Whether you think that something is worth its asking price is for you to decide.

For example, if you buy a pair of expensive jeans and pay more than the average price for them, you might expect them to last, to keep their shape and to wear well. Whereas if you buy a much cheaper pair, you may not worry if they go baggy in places and wear thin at the knees after a less time.

The right to redress

As a consumer you have the right to complain and to have your complaint settled fairly. This is called the right to redress.

Unfortunately, no matter how careful you may have been there's still a chance that something may go wrong. If it does then you may be entitled to ask for some, or maybe all, of your money back.

Consumer protection laws

Many of your rights as a consumer are backed by laws.

For example, your right to accurate information is protected by laws which demand the type of information that must be provided on certain products. Many foods have to list their ingredients, including any additives such as artificial colourings or preservatives.

The laws on your right to safety are very strict. They demand that suppliers must meet certain basic minimum standards.

Your right to redress is protected by laws that lay down the rules for fair and honest trading. They spell out the rights and obligations of suppliers and consumers.

Local councils have trading standards departments whose officers make sure that traders are not breaking the law. They regularly visit or check up on shops, and they investigate complaints made by the public.

In groups

Discuss what is meant by the right to redress. Tell each other about times when you have made a complaint about an item which you have bought. Do you think the complaint was dealt with fairly? Were you able to exchange the goods? Did you get your money back?

For your file

How responsible a shopper are you? Write a short statement saying how much you take your rights and responsibilities into account when you go shopping.

Developing your speaking skills: group discussions

As you grow up, it is important not only to develop your own ideas, but to learn to express them confidently and fluently.

Group discussions are a good way of developing your ideas, because you have the opportunity:

● to bounce your opinions off other people

● to consider different opinions by listening to other people's views

● to change your mind if you find their arguments convincing.

Guidelines for group discussions

Taking part in a group discussion is very different from having a chat with a friend. Below are some guidelines for you to follow, to help you to get the most out of your group discussions.

Taking part

When you take part in a group discussion:

Join in. Make sure you say something, even if you're not quite sure what your views are. It's difficult sometimes to know what you really think until you've tried to put your ideas into words. Trying out your ideas and seeing what other people think of them will help you to clarify them.

Listen carefully. Always listen when other people are speaking, even if you totally disagree with what they are saying. Try to pick out the reasons they give for their views, so that you can either agree or disagree with them when you speak. If someone says something you think is very important, it can be a good idea to note it down, so that you can refer back to it.

Wait your turn. Don't interrupt when someone else is still speaking, however much you disagree with what they are saying. Wait until they have finished and then have your say.

Give your reasons. Always try to back up your own views with your reasons. Wherever you can, quote facts and examples to support your statements. Explain why you disagree with other people's views.

Stick to the point. Keep to the subject under discussion. Don't start talking about other things or making clever comments just to get a laugh.

Chairing the discussion

Always appoint someone to chair the discussion. It is the chairperson's responsibility to organise and control the discussion.

A good chairperson will:

● start the discussion by reminding the group what the topic is;

● make sure that everyone gets a chance to speak;

● make sure that people wait their turn and do not interrupt others;

● keep the discussion focused on the task;

● suggest how to move the discussion forward if the group gets stuck;

● end the discussion by summarising what people have said.

In groups

Discuss what you learn from this page about taking part in and organising group discussions. Then study the articles on page 73 and discuss your views about battery hens.

Choose someone to report your different views to the rest of the class in a class discussion.

Should battery cages be banned?

There are over 300 million egg-laying hens in the European Union (EU) and more than three-quarters of them are confined in the barren battery cage system.

A battery hen spends her short life crammed into a small wire cage with several other hens. Until 2012 most battery hens were kept in barren battery cages, which prevented them from carrying out their natural behaviours such as foraging for food, laying their eggs in a nest, roosting, stretching their wings and dustbathing. As a result the hens suffered extreme physical and psychological stress.

Since January 2012, European legislation has required all battery cages to provide perches, a nest and a scratching area. The new cages are known as 'enriched' battery cages, but the total floor space allowed each bird remains very small.

It is hard for birds to move around and exercise. There is no minimum size of nest and scratch area, which is often just a small piece of Astroturf. There are no facilities for proper dustbathing and the position of perches can make it difficult for hens to move around and nest undisturbed.

Many people think that battery cages should be banned completely. They are willing to pay extra for free range eggs, which can cost twice as much, because they believe the hens are better cared for and much happier when they are not kept in battery cages.

Battery hens *'as happy as birds that can roam outside'*

Hens kept in battery cages are no more stressed than their free-range counterparts, researchers say.

These findings call into question the common belief that hens which are allowed to roam free are happier.

Similar amounts of a hormone produced when hens are frightened were found in the eggs of both kinds of hen.

Scientists believe this is because free-range hens have to deal with extra pressures such as extremes of temperature, more parasites and the threat of predators.

Dr Jeff Downing from Sydney University said, 'If they have no cover, they are constantly under fear of attack by predators. You can see it. A shadow comes over and they are completely startled.'

There are about 16 million caged hens in Britain, producing about half the eggs that are consumed annually.

Role play

Role play a studio discussion about keeping egg-laying hens in battery cages. Choose someone to be the presenter, who will chair the discussion, and two people to present the opposite views about battery hens – one a campaigner who is opposed to keeping them in cages, and another who argues that they should not be banned.

Start with the presenter asking the two people about their views, before inviting the members of the audience to express their opinions.

Developing your speaking skills: making a speech

Sometimes you will be asked to act as the reporter and to present your group's views to the rest of the class. You will also be asked to prepare a speech expressing your own views and opinions on a particular subject. It is important, therefore, to develop the skills you need to speak to an audience.

Preparing your speech

First, you need to think about what your views are and why. A good way of sorting out what you think on a topic is to draw up a list of the arguments for and against a particular point of view.

Tony was asked to give a speech saying whether he thought boxing should be banned. Look at the start of his list of arguments (right).

Boxing should be banned

For:	Against:
People can get badly hurt. They may get brain damage. Boxers can die after being KO'd.	Boxing's no more dangerous than many other sports. You can get paralysed or killed playing rugby.

Helpful Hint

If you are stuck for arguments on a topic, go to the library or resources centre and see what information you can find on it in books and articles, on television and on the Internet. You can also use the resources centre to check facts, as well as to provide you with evidence and examples to support the arguments you are going to use.

In groups

Discuss people's views about boxing, and draw up a list of other arguments for and against boxing.

Share your views on blood sports and draw up a list of arguments for and against making blood sports illegal.

Planning your speech

A good way to plan your speech is to make a flow-chart. This helps you to plan the order in which to put your ideas. Here is the flow-chart that Prisha made when planning a speech giving her views on zoos.

For your file

What are your views on zoos? Use the resources centre to find out more about zoos and people's views on them. Then draw your own flow-chart and write a speech giving your views on zoos.

Introduction: Zoos are cruel. Animals should be free, not caged.

↓

However well designed enclosures are, they are no substitute for natural habitats.

↓

Conditions at zoos (especially small ones) are often awful.

↓

Many zoo animals show signs of abnormal behaviour from being locked up.

↓

It's said zoos are educational but you can learn more from TV wildlife programmes.

↓

Experts argue they can study animals in zoos, but they can do that in the wild.

↓

Conclusion: Zoos exploit animals for human entertainment.

Delivering your speech

How effective your speech is will depend not only on how good your arguments are but also on how well you deliver it.

On the right is a list of things you need to think about when making your speech.

In groups

Discuss the advice that is given on this page about how to deliver your speeches, and say what you think the three most important pieces of advice are.

Take it in turns to deliver a speech to the class about a topic on which you've got strong opinions. At the end of each speech give the speaker marks out of ten for the delivery of their speech. Discuss what was good about the way they delivered their speech, and what they could do to improve their delivery next time they give a speech.

1 Look at the audience. It's important to keep eye-contact with the audience. Looking at them helps to keep their attention. So don't spend all the time looking down at your notes.

2 Speak up. Speak loudly enough so that everyone can hear you, but don't shout. It's difficult to concentrate if someone is shouting.

3 Speak clearly. Make sure you speak clearly and don't mumble. Your listeners aren't likely to be convinced by your arguments if they have to strain to work out what you're saying.

4 Use plenty of expression. Vary the tone of your voice. For example, speak loudly to emphasise how strongly you feel about something. If you speak in the same tone of voice throughout your speech, the audience may get bored.

5 Don't speak too fast. Speak at a normal pace. If you go too slowly, your audience may 'switch off'. If you speak too fast, the chances are that they won't be able to follow what you're saying.

6 Speak fluently. Try to avoid saying 'um' and 'er' too much. It can be very distracting to listen to.

7 Stand up straight. However nervous you feel, don't show it by slouching. Your body language should suggest that you are confident. It can be effective to use hand gestures to emphasise particular points, but don't overdo them as they can be distracting.

Developing your writing skills

You can express your opinions in writing in a number of ways – for example, in an essay, in a magazine article or in a email to a newspaper. Whichever form you use, it's important to plan your writing and to think carefully about how you are going to develop your argument.

Writing an email to a newspaper

In my opinion

Subject: Toy guns
From: Zarah

I think that toy guns and weapons should be banned. They give young children the wrong idea. It suggests that war is fun and violence is OK.

Some people say that playing war games is harmless and that it helps people let off steam. They say that it gets rid of aggressive feelings that might otherwise lead to real violence. I don't agree. If you play violent games, you're more likely to act violently.

Besides, it's nearly always boys who want to play war games and it's boys who become soldiers and fight wars. So I say, stop encouraging them and ban toy weapons.

Subject: Falling for the latest fashion
From: Tristan

Why do so many people follow fashions? Don't they realise what's really going on? It's all a big con. They are being tricked into buying things just because everyone else is.

Why do they fall for these crazy crazes? One minute it's Vans, the next it's Nikes. Can't they see they are being manipulated by the marketing men?

Why not show some individuality for a change and resist the temptation to be like everybody else? Wear a T-shirt you dyed yourself instead of one showing the latest Disney or games console character. And spend your money on something useful rather than a plastic model of a mermaid or an alien!

Subject: Football crazy
From: Abi

Why are so many people obsessed with football? They spend all their time talking about it, reading about it, and watching it on TV. You'd think it was really important, the way they go on about it.

And another thing. Why are football players paid so much? It's totally ridiculous the amount some of them get each week. As for the size of transfer fees, they're absurd!

Also, there are far too many foreign players in British football. Clubs should spend their time developing local talent instead of importing stars from abroad.

I think we've all gone football crazy.

In groups

Study the emails (left), written by teens to a newspaper for young people. Imagine you had to choose one of the emails to win a £15 prize as Email of the Week. Consider the points listed below, and decide which email you would choose and why.

- Which email has the most effective opening?
- In which email is the main statement best supported by the arguments that are developed and the evidence that is quoted?
- Which email has the most effective ending?
- Which email involves the reader the most?

For your file

Which of the arguments in these emails do you agree or disagree with most strongly? Write a reply to one of the emails stating your views on the subject.

Writing an article or essay

Following these steps will help you plan and write your article or essay effectively.

1 Find out
as much as you can about your subject by reading up on it in books and magazines. Go to the resources centre, read up about it in reference books and use the Internet to visit any websites that might be useful.

2 Make notes
of any key facts you might want to use in your argument, or things people have said that you agree or disagree with. Always keep a record of where you found the information.

3 Make a plan
Do a brainstorm and list all the points you are going to make. Then number them to show the order in which you are going to make them.

4 State your viewpoint
clearly in the first paragraph. Start with a statement or a question that will grab your readers' attention.

5 Explain the reasons
for your opinions.

6 Use evidence and examples
to support your statements.

7 Give the source
of any key facts that you include, and the names of any people whose statements you quote.

8 End with a statement
that either sums up your argument or recommends any action you think needs to be taken.

Here is the plan that Dominic made before writing an article saying that he thinks we should stop celebrating Bonfire Night.

Paragraph 1 – Bonfire Night celebrations are out of date and should be stopped.

Paragraph 2 – Celebrating by burning a guy is the wrong way to remember the barbaric custom of burning people at the stake.

Paragraph 3 – Every year bonfires get out of control. Nov 5th is the fire brigade's busiest night of the year.

Paragraph 4 – Every year there are lots of firework accidents (e.g. boy with horrific facial burns in November 2012).

Paragraph 5 – Bonfire Night is terrifying for animals.

Paragraph 6 – People say it's traditional and gives enjoyment. That's no reason to keep it.

Paragraph 7 – So Bonfire Night should be scrapped. Instead of spending money on fireworks, give it to a good cause.

For your file

Write an article for a magazine for young people either on a subject on which you have strong opinions or on one of the following questions:

- Should parents be allowed to smack children?
- Has Christmas lost its true meaning?
- Is it right to ban fox hunting?

What is a healthy diet?

Healthy Eating Facts

"The key to looking and feeling great is to enjoy yourself, and that means eating what you like in sensible amounts."

To keep healthy you need to eat a balanced diet. Your body needs some body-building foods (proteins), some energy-giving foods (carbohydrates and fats) and some protective foods (vitamins and minerals). It also needs plenty of fibre, which helps you to get rid of solid waste.

Foods that contain proteins include: meat and fish, milk, cheese and eggs, and plant foods such as peas, soya beans and peanuts.

Foods that contain carbohydrates include: bread, potatoes, pasta, cereals and rice. You also get energy from foods that contain fats, such as milk, butter, cheese, margarine and vegetable oils.

Foods that contain vitamins and fibre include: fresh fruit and vegetables. Wholewheat bread, cereals and pasta all contain plenty of fibre.

By eating a range of these different foods you will also get the small amounts of minerals your body needs.

The right amount

Your body needs the right amount of food. If you eat too much or too little, you are likely to get ill. In Britain many people eat too much fat, sugar and salt. Research has shown that there are links between what we eat and many modern diseases. For example, a healthy diet cuts down your chances of developing heart trouble.

In groups

Discuss what you learn from the article 'What is a healthy diet?' about the different foods that your body needs.

What does the article say about eating the right amount of food? Which foods do many people in Britain eat too much of?

Brown-bread egg and cress sandwiches

Banana

Muesli bar

Bottle of flavoured water

Francesca

Hamburger in a white bun with onions and mayonnaise

Large portion of fries

Large cola

Sam

Portion of chips

Apple pie and custard

Glass of tap water

Darren

Fish fingers, carrots and boiled potatoes

Jelly and ice cream

Carton of orange juice

Lauren

In groups

Study what the four children had for lunch (left).

Who do you think had the most healthy lunch – Francesca, Darren, Sam or Lauren? Who had the least healthy lunch?

Each write down what you had for lunch either today or yesterday. Discuss what each of you had, and decide who had the most healthy lunch.

In pairs

Design a leaflet offering advice to other students on what to eat at lunchtime. If the school has a canteen, you could offer advice on what to choose to have as a healthy school dinner, as well as on what you should have in a healthy packed lunch.

eating and exercise

Are you eating a healthy diet?

TRUDY'S EATING DIARY

I'm not sure how healthy my diet is. I don't eat much fruit and I don't like many vegetables. I like chocolate biscuits and cake. I don't like fish and I prefer chicken to other kinds of meat. But I do like chips! Here's what I had to eat this week:

SATURDAY

Breakfast: Cereal
Mid-morning: Chocolate biscuits
Lunch: Chicken burger and chips
Tea: Cake
Supper: Ham sandwich, orange juice

SUNDAY

Breakfast: Egg on toast, orange juice
Lunch: Chicken and chips
Tea: Cake, ice cream
Supper: Spaghetti

MONDAY

Breakfast: Orange juice
Mid-morning: Crisps
Lunch: Sausages and chips
Tea: Banana
Supper: Egg and beans on toast

TUESDAY

Mid-morning: Chocolate biscuits
Lunch: Cheese roll and crisps
Tea: Toast
Supper: Pizza

WEDNESDAY

Breakfast: Toast, orange juice
Mid-morning: Crisps
Lunch: Ham roll, banana
Tea: Cake
Supper: Cheese on toast, soup

THURSDAY

Breakfast: Orange juice
Mid-morning: Chocolate biscuits
Lunch: Pizza and chips
Tea: Banana
Supper: Beans on toast

FRIDAY

Mid-morning: Crisps
Lunch: Cheese roll, chocolate biscuit
Tea: Cake
Supper: Chicken curry

In pairs

Discuss what Trudy eats. What do you think are the plus points about her diet? What are the minus points about her diet? What advice would you give her? Write down what you think she could do to improve her diet. Then share your ideas in a group discussion.

For your file

Keep a food diary. Write down everything you eat each day for a week. Then write a comment saying whether or not you think you eat a healthy diet, and anything you think you need to do to improve your diet.

Healthy Eating Tips

1 Have a proper breakfast each morning, but eat plain breakfast cereals rather than sugar-coated ones.
2 Eat brown bread rather than white bread.
3 Drink fresh fruit juice rather than cola or lemonade.
4 Have a piece of fruit or some unsalted nuts as a snack rather than crisps, sweets or chocolate.
5 Add herbs and spices for flavour rather than salt.
6 Eat more fish and chicken and less red meat.
7 Have a jacket potato or boiled potatoes rather than chips.
8 Use spread rather than butter on your bread.

In groups

Discuss the reasons for each of the healthy eating tips. Try to add some more tips to the list.

'People under 16 should be banned from eating unhealthy foods.' Say why you agree or disagree with this idea.

Why is exercise important?

Exercise keeps you fit and healthy and helps you to feel good. It's important to take exercise regularly, at least three times a week. For the exercise to be effective, you need to do it for long enough – at least 20 minutes – and hard enough, until you are breathing heavily.

Some good reasons for taking exercise

 Exercise builds up your **stamina** or staying power – your ability to keep going without feeling out of breath.

 Exercise helps to keep your **lungs** in good condition. When you exercise you breathe more quickly and deeply, because you need more energy and use up more oxygen.

 Exercise builds up your **strength** by developing your muscles and keeping them in good working order.

 Exercise helps to make your **heart** work more efficiently. It improves your circulation because it increases the rate at which the blood flows round the body. Exercise helps to protect people against heart disease.

 Exercise develops your **suppleness**. If you are supple, you can bend and stretch your body easily, and you are less likely to injure yourself.

 Exercise can help you to control your **weight**. It uses up the calories in food that might otherwise be stored as fat.

 Exercise helps you to **relax**. It is a good way of getting rid of tension, when you feel stressed.

Swimming is a good form of exercise. You use lots of muscles, and it builds up your strength and suppleness as well as your stamina.

You can also get exercise by taking the dog for a brisk walk. You don't have to be a sports fanatic to be healthy.

Role play

Act out a scene in which someone who believes that exercise is good for you argues with someone who says that exercise is a waste of time.

In pairs

Are you getting enough exercise? Each keep an exercise diary for a week. At the end of the week, discuss how much exercise you have each done. Then, each set yourself a 'fitness target', for example, 'In four weeks' time I shall be able to swim 30 lengths of the pool.' Do not be too ambitious. Set yourself a target that you have a good chance of achieving.

In groups

Produce a leaflet explaining what sports and activities are available for people of your age in your area – for example, at the leisure centre, at your school and at sports clubs.

Exercise and body shape

Some young people are unhappy with their body shape, so they start to diet. But if you want to improve your body shape, a much better way is to eat a balanced, healthy diet and take exercise.

Your body shape depends on a number of factors, such as your bone structure and the rate at which your body burns up the energy in the food you eat. This is known as your metabolic rate.

Different people have slightly different metabolic rates. If you have a faster rate, you may be able to eat a lot without gaining fat because you use the calories quickly. If you have a slower metabolic rate, you may burn up food more slowly and gain fat more easily. If you exercise regularly, your metabolic rate will be permanently increased.

Olympic gold medallist athlete Jessica Ennis-Hill believes some girls are afraid of taking up sport in case it makes them look too muscular. They fear that training will change their body shape making them look unattractive and different. "I'm always saying that strong can look good," she says.

Losing weight

There is a lot of pressure nowadays, especially on girls and women, to conform to a certain shape. The models you see in magazines are usually thin. This may make people worry about their weight. People weigh different amounts because they have different builds. A short, stocky person may weigh more than a tall, skinny person. Men tend to weigh more than women because they have more muscle on their bodies, which is a heavy tissue.

You do not need to lose weight unless you are storing so much extra fat on your body that it might strain your heart and be bad for you. If you are anxious about this, you should ask your doctor whether you should go on a controlled diet.

Going on a diet

Think carefully before you start to diet. Remember:

▶ It's never worth going on a strict diet unless you're seriously overweight. Your doctor can tell you if you really do need to lose weight, and will recommend a sensible, healthy diet and exercise plan.

▶ As you start to grow older your body goes through puberty. It's natural to fill out a bit more and become curvy. This is a sign that your body is maturing – it doesn't mean that you're becoming fat!

▶ It's never a good idea to ban any particular food. Once you decide you're not going to eat chocolate again, for instance, you'll suddenly find that you want it more than anything else in the world.

▶ If you feel hungry, eat! It's natural to have a big appetite as you go through puberty because your body uses up a lot of energy in developing.

▶ Talking to someone about your feelings over food can really help. Choose someone you think will be sympathetic and understanding.

In groups

Discuss whether boys are also pressurised to conform to a certain shape. (Look at male body images in magazines.) What effect may this pressure have on boys?

For your file

Write a letter to a magazine complaining about the way that the adverts in the magazine only show thin models.

Government

Britain's system of government is a parliamentary democracy. In a democracy all the adults have the opportunity to choose the people who form the government. In Britain, there is a general election at which people vote for a person to represent them in Parliament. A general election has to be held at least once every five years.

What is Parliament?

Parliament is the name given to the body of people who make laws and take decisions on behalf of the British people. It consists of the House of Commons, which is composed of the Members of Parliament (MPs) elected at general elections, the House of Lords and the reigning king or queen, known as the sovereign or monarch.

Who runs Parliament?

In the past, the sovereign and the House of Lords were more powerful than the House of Commons.

Today, the real power lies with the House of Commons. The powers of the House of Lords are strictly limited. It can only delay for a year any new law that the House of Commons wants to make, and it has no control over financial measures, which have to pass through the House of Lords without being voted on.

The sovereign now has only a formal role in the government of the country. New sessions of Parliament are opened by the sovereign, and before a general election can be held the sovereign 'dissolves' the existing Parliament on the advice of the Prime Minister. The sovereign has to give approval to any new laws, but never refuses to do so.

For your file

Use the Internet to research how power has, over the centuries, passed from the monarch and the House of Lords to the House of Commons, so that Britain has become a parliamentary democracy. Draw a timeline from 1215 to the present, showing the key landmarks in this shift, such as Magna Carta, The 1689 Bill of Rights, the 1832 Reform Act, the 1911 Parliament Act, the 1918 Representation of the People Act, the 1949 Parliament Act.

What does Parliament do?

- It makes news laws for the United Kingdom and examines proposals for new laws being introduced in the European Union.
- It questions government ministers about their policies and challenges government decisions.
- It controls the nation's finances, deciding what taxes to collect and how to spend the nation's money.
- It protects the rights of individual citizens. Anyone who feels unfairly treated by the government can ask their MP to take up their case.
- It holds debates on matters of national and international importance, such as the UK's relations with a particular foreign country.

Parliament and government

The government is responsible for running the country. It decides policy and drafts new laws.

Parliament is responsible for checking the work of government and for debating and passing all laws.

What happens after a general election

- A general election is held
- The Queen invites the leader of the political party with the most MPs to form a government.
- A government is formed either from the members of a party with an overall majority of MPs or a coalition of parties and the leader of the party with the most MPs becomes Prime Minister.
- The Prime Minister appoints senior politicians as ministers to run particular government departments.
- Senior ministers meet together as the Cabinet to decide on what the government's policies are and what new laws are needed.
- The Queen as head of state opens Parliament and announces the government's plans.

What is the Civil Service?

The Civil Service is responsible for putting government policies into practice. It is split into departments each of which is attached to a government department. Civil servants are not members of any political party. They advise ministers and assist in the drafting of new laws.

In pairs

Prepare a Test Yourself quiz about how Britain is governed, consisting of a number of true or false statements based on the information given on these page. Then get another pair to complete it.

The Role of the Monarchy

What is constitutional monarchy?

The United Kingdom is a constitutional monarchy – a form of government in which a king or queen acts as the Head of State.

The ability to make and pass legislation resides with an elected Parliament, not the monarch.

As a system of government, constitutional monarchy separates the Head of State's ceremonial and official duties from party politics.

A constitutional monarchy also provides stability, continuity and a national focus, as the Head of State remains the same even as governments change.

The Sovereign/Monarch governs according to the constitution – that is according to rules rather than according to his or her own free will. The United Kingdom does not have a written constitution which sets out the rights and duties of the Sovereign, they are established by conventions. These are non-statutory rules which can be just as binding as formal constitutional rules.

As a constitutional monarch, the Sovereign must remain politically neutral.

On almost all matters, the Sovereign acts on the advice of ministers. However, the Sovereign retains an important political role as Head of State, formally appointing prime ministers, approving certain legislation and bestowing honours.

The Sovereign has other official roles to play such as Head of the Armed Forces.

From *The British Monarchy* website

In groups

Discuss the role that the monarchy plays in the government of the UK.

Some people think that the monarchy should be scrapped. Discuss these views and say why you agree or disagree with them.

"**The monarchy has no place in a modern democracy.**"

"**It costs millions of pounds a year of taxpayers' money to support the monarchy.**"

"**If we didn't have a monarch we'd have to have an elected president. It wouldn't be the same as having a royal family.**"

"**The monarch represents tradition and fulfils a necessary role in Britain's government because the monarch is non-political.**"

"**Though the monarch is said to be impartial, too much publicity is given to the views expressed by members of the royal family. The monarchy should be abolished.**"

"**We'd lose some of our national identify, if we didn't have a monarch.**"

The European Union

The UK is a member of the European Union, a group of 27 countries that have decided to share power. The main idea of the EU was to create a common market. In this market, all goods, services and labour can be freely traded across the whole of the EU.

The EU can make laws which are adopted in all the countries that are members. It is estimated that about 15% of new laws in the UK are made by the EU.

Regional government

Since 1998 the House of Commons has had less power than it used to. Elected bodies have been set up with the power to make decisions affecting the people of Scotland, Wales and Northern Ireland. The process of transferring power from a central government to regional governments is known as devolution.

The **Scottish Parliament** is based in Edinburgh. It has powers over many areas of Scottish life, including regional policy and health and education spending. It can make new laws and is responsible for the law and home affairs in Scotland.

The largest party in the Scottish Parliament after the 2011 election is the Scottish Nationalist Party. In 2014, there will be a referendum on whether Scotland should be independent.

The **Northern Ireland Assembly** is based in Belfast. It has 108 members and an executive consisting of representatives of all the political parties. It controls the economic development of Northern Ireland and makes laws and policy in areas such as health, education and social security.

The **Welsh Assembly** is based in Cardiff. It has responsibilities for education, health authorities and local government in Wales. It cannot, however, set taxes

The Scottish Parliament

The Welsh Assembly

In groups

Use the internet to research the arguments for and against an independent Scotland. Then organise a debate on the motion 'This house believes that Scotland should remain part of the United Kingdom'.

What is work?

Three teenagers discuss their views on what work is.

Sam: I think work is anything you do that you get paid money for doing.

Tara: But there are other kinds of work. What about housework and things like doing the garden?

Amrit: Yes – and schoolwork. You don't get paid for that! And there's voluntary work. My grandmother's retired but she does voluntary work at a local care home for older people. She only gets her expenses paid, like if she drives one of the old people somewhere.

Tara: There are different kinds of work too. Like whether you're employed or self-employed.

Amrit: And what about being unemployed and doing a training course? That's work isn't it?

Sam: And there's part-time work, such as doing a Saturday job or doing three evenings a week. Not everyone works full-time.

Tara: Some people talk about blue collar workers and white collar workers. What do they mean?

Amrit: It depends on the job they do. Factory workers and tradesmen, like carpenters, are blue collar workers. People like office workers and professional people are white collar workers.

Sam: And you can talk about manual workers – people who do things or make things with their hands.

Amrit: Yes, but that's separating physical and mental work. I think work is any activity that involves making a physical or mental effort, whether you are paid for it or not.

 In groups

Discuss these teenagers' views on work. Write down your own definition of work. Compare your definitions in a class discussion.

Why do people work?

People work for lots of different reasons.

To get money

Most people work for money. They need money to spend on essentials, like food and housing, and on leisure activities that they enjoy. If you work in a job and pay your taxes, you work in what is called the formal economy. The money that you earn for your work is called wages.

Some people work in return for being given their food or accommodation, or in return for favours. This is called working in the informal economy.

To gain work experience

Some jobs require you to have done something before. This is known as work experience. For example, you can't just become a computer operator. You need to have some experience of using computers.

To gain a qualification

Some jobs require you to have a qualification. For example, a teacher can't just come into a school and teach. They need a teaching qualification in order to be able to do this.

To benefit society

Some people choose to do jobs not for the money, but because they benefit society. Those who join the police force or the fire service may do so for this reason. Other people work as volunteers for no money, in order to help people out.

To do something that interests them

Other people work in particular careers because the work interests them. But what is interesting to one person may be boring to another. Some people like working in gardens, others like working indoors on computers. It all depends on the type of work you enjoy.

Case study

Fred works as a volunteer firefighter. These are firefighters who help fight fires in rural areas, where the job is only occasional and part time.

"I don't just do it for the money," explains Fred. "I also do it because I enjoy giving something back to the local community. It's also good to be part of a team."

"However, there are disadvantages," adds Fred. "You have to be ready to fight a fire any time day or night. The alarm can go off at any time. Once I had to get up and be ready within 2 minutes at 5 am in the morning. My wife didn't like it at the time. But she understands it's something I really enjoy, so she puts up with it."

In pairs

Discuss Fred's job. What advantages and disadvantages does he mention? Would you ever consider being a volunteer firefighter?

The advantages and disadvantages of work

While there are often many advantages you may get from working, work may also have disadvantages too.

Balancing your time

Work means that you are busy and can't do other things. How many times have you wanted to go out and play when there is homework to do? The same is true for adults who work, but want to have leisure time too.

People now talk about a work/life balance. This means making sure that they are doing enough work to provide themselves with the money that they need. But it also means that they have enough time to enjoy themselves with their friends or family.

Variety versus boredom

Some work is repetitive and may become boring. For example, if you are stacking supermarket shelves, you have to repeat the same activity day after day. If you are a heating engineer, you will spend the week servicing and repairing people's boilers.

But not all boilers are the same. When one breaks down, you'll have to work out what's wrong with it. So a job can be both repetitive and varied.

Working on your own

An increasing number of people are self-employed. This means that they work for themselves. They have the advantage of being able to decide for themselves when they work, how long they work and what they do.

But working on your own has its drawbacks too. They may be worried about making enough money and may take on too much work, so they get stressed. And they don't get holiday pay or paid when they are ill.

Working with others

If you work as part of a team, you get the advantage of having contact with other people. Many workers make friends with some of the people they work with.

But you will also have a manager to tell you what to do. This has its advantages and disadvantages. If you have a problem you can discuss it with them. But you may not like having to do what the manager says.

Getting stressed

Some jobs are more stressful than others. It often depends on how much responsibility you have. If you are the manager of a shop, you may have to work long hours and have targets to meet. But if you are a shop assistant, you can go home at the end of your shift without having to worry about what the weekly takings were.

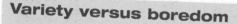

In pairs

Choose a repetitive job, such as working on a supermarket checkout or as a packer in a factory. Draw up a list of the advantages and disadvantages of the job, then compare your views with those of another pair.

What do you think are the advantages and disadvantages of **a)** working with others **b)** being self-employed?

For your file

Think about a job that a friend or family member does. Write a short report for your file. Is it full time or part time? Is it paid or voluntary? Why do they do the job? What are the advantages and disadvantages of the job?

What do you want from work?

What do you value most? Are you looking for a career that gives you the most status in society or that pays you the most money? Or are you looking for a job that you'll be really interested in doing or that benefits society?

Here's what a group of young people said when asked what they would want from a job:

> **"I'd like a job with prospects – one that gives you training and there's an opportunity for you to start at the bottom and move up."**

> **"I'm not too bothered about whether the job's repetitive and boring, so long as the money's good."**

> **"I want a job that's interesting. I'd be prepared to work for less money than I might get doing a different job in order to do something that I liked doing."**

> **"I don't want a job that means I'd be working on my own all the time. I want a job that involves working alongside other people or meeting new people."**

> **"I couldn't stand being indoors all the time, like working in an office. I want a job that means you're working outdoors or travelling from place to place."**

> **"I'd be prepared to do lots of studying, if it means that I'd end up by being qualified to do a highly paid job."**

> **"I'd do anything, even if it meant getting only the minimum wage, rather than being unemployed and having nothing to do all day."**

> **"I want a job that means I'd be helping people in some way. Job satisfaction is very important to me."**

> **"I want a job without too much responsibility, so that I don't end up worrying about work all the time."**

In groups

Study what these people say they want from work. Is there anything they *don't* say that is important to you? Write two or three sentences about what you would want from work, then share your views in a group or class discussion.

Choosing a charity

One way you can help the community is by raising money for a charity.
First of all, you have to decide which charity to choose.

Name: Oxfam
Founded: 1942

Oxfam works with poor communities overseas by funding programmes for development and relief run by local people. Today there are 11 organisations around the world that make up Oxfam International, working to overcome poverty and suffering. Oxfam campaigns on issues such as debt, education and trade. The first charity shop in the UK was an Oxfam shop; now Oxfam has a chain of shops. It also promotes fair trade by supporting producers around the world, and selling food and craft goods in Oxfam shops.

Name: The National Trust
Founded: 1895

The National Trust for Places of Historic Interest or Natural Beauty is a charity that preserves countryside and buildings in England, Wales and Northern Ireland for the benefit of us all. The Trust now has about 300 historic houses, castles and gardens which it opens to the public. It also owns over 244,000 hectares of open countryside, such as large parts of the Lake District, and protects over 575 miles of unspoilt coastline. These stretches of country are permanently available to the public.

Name: Mind
Founded: 1946

Mind is the leading mental health charity in England and Wales, working for a better life for everyone with experience of emotional distress. Mind promotes mental health awareness and the development of community services through more than 200 local associations. It also fights discrimination against those with mental health issues. Mind offers a full range of publications, a bimonthly magazine, a free quarterly newsletter and a programme of conferences and training. MindinfoLine, the charity's national information service, covers all aspects of mental health.

Name: Scope
Founded: 1952

Scope is the UK's leading charity working with disabled people, their families and carers. It was formed by parents of children with cerebral palsy to fight for better services and opportunities. Scope has developed partnerships with over 280 voluntary groups throughout England and Wales, which have grown up in response to the needs of their communities. The charity also opens doors for people with cerebral palsy through specialist schools, its further education college and its cerebral palsy helpline. Scope also provides opportunities to increase independence through employment schemes, skill development centres and residential support services.

Name: **WWF-UK**
Founded: **1961**

The World Wide Fund For Nature is the world's largest conservation organisation, which works to preserve the world's nature and wildlife. WWF-UK, the British national branch, currently operates projects throughout the world, and runs a programme of policy work and field projects on UK and European issues. Its recent Vanishing Species campaign focuses on the mountain gorilla. Its Climate Change campaign helped to convince the government to set a target of reducing all greenhouse gas emissions by 80% by 2050 in the Climate Change Act 2005. The WWF also funds a wide education programme.

Name: **RNLI**
Founded: **1824**

The Royal National Lifeboat Institution is a charity which exists to save lives at sea. It provides, on call, the 24-hour service necessary to cover search and rescue requirements to 50 miles out from the coast of the United Kingdom and the Republic of Ireland. There are more than 220 lifeboat stations and their lifeboats launch more than 6,000 times a year, saving on average 1,300 lives. They are manned by highly trained volunteer crews. Every penny required to maintain the lifeboat service is raised from voluntary contributions and legacies.

Name: **Guide Dogs for the Blind Association**
Founded: **1934**

The Guide Dogs for the Blind Association provides guide dogs and other services that meet the needs of blind and partially sighted people. Whatever one's age, whatever the condition, sight loss causes a huge adjustment to everyday routines and activities. Above all, it can mean a severe loss of mobility. The Guide Dogs for the Blind Association helps people rebuild their lives and literally find a sense of direction with the assistance of a specially trained guide and companion. Since guide dogs don't suit everyone, the charity also provides training with a long cane and a variety of other techniques.

Name: **Shelter**
Founded: **1966**

Shelter

Shelter (The housing and homelessness charity) aims to provide decent, secure and affordable housing as a basic human right. To achieve this, Shelter carries out a range of campaigning activities and provides practical advice services for badly housed and homeless people. The charity supports a network of over 60 housing aid centres and projects throughout England. Housing aid workers provide advice and assistance on homelessness, benefits, housing debt and other housing problems. Shelter also operates Shelterline, which provides freephone telephone advice to anyone with a housing problem.

In groups

Imagine that the school is organising a charity week. Your class has been asked to choose two charities which the school is going to support from a shortlist of ten charities.

Study the information about the eight charities given on these pages and decide your first and second choices of charity. Then draft a statement to explain to the rest of the class why you have chosen those two charities. Share your views in a class discussion and hold a vote to decide which two charities your class would recommend supporting.

Raising money for a charity

These two pages explain how you can work together as a class to raise money for a local charity. You could raise money for the local branch of a national charity, such as one of the charities described on pages 94–95, or for a different charity altogether.

Alternatively, your local hospital may need money for a new piece of equipment, or the local day centre for older people may need money to help fund the trips and outings that it organises.

Fundraising activities

There are various ways you could raise money:

Organise a sponsored event, such as a sponsored silence or a sponsored walk

Hold a sale of second-hand toys and books

Run a stall at a local fete

Put on an evening's entertainment

Make something to sell, for example, Christmas cards

In groups

Discuss which local charity you think you should support. Choose a spokesperson to explain your views to the rest of the class in a class discussion. Then hold a vote to decide which one you are going to support.

In groups

Discuss your ideas for a fundraising event. Then share your ideas in a class discussion and hold a vote to decide what your fundraising activity is going to be.

Organising a fundraising event

The first thing you need to do when planning your fundraising event is to make a list of all the jobs that will need doing. Once you have done that, you need to appoint people to do the various tasks.

Group in charge of the room(s)

Responsible for:
- getting permission to use the buildings where the sale is to be held
- making sure the buildings will be open and then locked up afterwards
- setting up the room and making sure it is cleared up and cleaned afterwards.

Group in charge of publicity

Responsible for:
- drafting and sending out letters to people, telling them that you need second-hand toys and books, when they will be collected and where they can be delivered to;
- designing and producing posters to advertise the sale.

Group in charge of collection

Responsible for organising the collection of the toys and books.

Group in charge of the toys and books

Responsible for storing, sorting and pricing the toys and books.

Group in charge of the sale

Responsible for organising the actual sale, e.g. arranging for a rota of people to be at each of the different tables and for parents and teachers to act as adult volunteers to help to sell the goods and collect the money.

In groups

Make a list of all the jobs that will have to be done in order for the event to take place. Then share your ideas and make a complete list of everything that needs to be done. You need to decide who is going to do each job.

You could appoint small groups of people to work together. One class, which decided to hold a sale of second-hand toys and books, set up five groups. Each group had a different responsibility (see left).

The planning committee

You could appoint a planning committee consisting of all the group leaders. The advantage of having a committee is that it can check everything has been done and discuss how to deal with any problems that arise.

Presenting your donation

After the event, invite someone from the organisation you have chosen to support to come to the school to be presented with the money you have raised. You could ask them to give a short talk about the work the organisation does and how the money will be used.

Reviewing the event

After the event, hold a class discussion. Talk about what went well, the problems you faced while organising it and how you coped with them. What were the strengths and weaknesses of how you organised the event? What lessons did you learn? How would you organise things differently, if you were to run a similar event in the future?

For your file

Write a report for the school newsletter about the event, saying what you did, why you chose to support that charity and how much money you raised.

Disability

Defining disability

Here is a dictionary definition:

dĭsabĭ'lĭtў A disability is a physical or mental incapacity or illness that restricts someone's way of life

Compare it with this definition produced by disabled people:

Disability: the disadvantage caused when society takes little or no account of people having physical impairments and thus excludes them from participating fully in everyday social activities.

What is a disability?

A disability is often described as an impairment or medical condition which prevents someone from performing a specific task or function.

However, many people consider that it is not the impairment itself which is disabling, but the fact that society often limits the opportunities available to disabled people. An impairment may be caused by the loss of part or all of a limb, or by an organ or mechanism of the body not working properly. A physical impairment affects the working of the body. A learning impairment or difficulty restricts a person's mental development. People become disabled when, as a result of their impairment, they are faced with physical and social barriers that make it difficult for them to participate fully within the community.

In groups

Discuss what we mean by disability. Ask yourselves: If you are a wheelchair-user faced with a set of steps, what disables you most – your wheelchair or the design of the building?

Becoming disabled

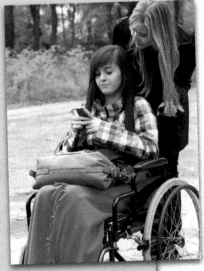

There are all kinds of impairments that make people differently able.

Each person is unique. People with the same kind of impairment may be affected in different ways and to varying degrees.

Some conditions that cause an impairment are passed down from parent to child. These are genetic or hereditary conditions. Others may be caused by the body not growing properly, or by disease. Many are the result of accidents.

Most disabilities are permanent, although their nature as well as the needs of the disabled person may change. For instance, someone who has had a stroke may at first be seriously disabled. This may improve in time. With specialist support, someone with a learning disability is often able to overcome some of his or her difficulties. The majority of disabled people are not ill, although some will have medical conditions that do affect their health.

In groups

Use the Internet to research and write a set of factsheets about the most common medical conditions that can cause physical or mental impairment: autism, brain damage, cerebral palsy, cystic fibrosis, Down's Syndrome, epilepsy, multiple sclerosis, muscular dystrophy, sensory impairments (deafness, loss of sight, speech impairments), spina bifida, spinal injury, stroke.

people with disabilities

What is it like to have a disability?

Here are some comments made by young people with disabilities about their lives and how they feel about people's attitudes towards them.

> "I am the same as you in that I can hear, learn and reason out things like you. I breathe like you. I feel hungry like you and I have needs and wishes like you.
>
> I'm different from you in that my limbs are not as strong as yours and I am not able to do some of the manual work which you are able to do." **Mwaniki**

> "There are many things I'd like all able-bodied children to understand. I would like them to know that just because there is something wrong with my spine it does not mean my brain is affected. I wish they would understand that being in a wheelchair does not make me any different from them." **Heather**

> "I am not my disability, I'm me. I have dyslexia and I've had polio, but I'm not a 'dyslexic' or 'a cripple', I'm me." **John**

> "I don't want your pity. You think that just because we have a problem with our vision that we can't do things for ourselves, but we all are equal. And why did they give the title 'handicap'? Do you know how offensive that is?" **Maureen**

> "Sometimes I envy those who can go to restaurants and can feed themselves, while I have to depend on others to feed me. I also notice people often stare at me, or have a pitiful look on their faces. Personally I don't like people taking pity on me when I am no different from anyone else." **Cathy**

> "I see through your eyes pity for me
> I don't want your pity or your lies
> You see my chair instead of me
> You see many things wrong with me
> instead of just me."
> **Colleen**

In groups

What do you learn from these comments about the way young people with disabilities feel about how able-bodied people treat them? How do they want to be treated?

Think about how we speak about disability. Study the lists of words on the right. Which are more positive and why?

A	B
The disabled, the handicapped, the blind	Disabled people, people with disabilities, people who are blind
Wheelchair-bound	Wheelchair user
Suffering from, victim of …	Person who has …
Spastic	Person with cerebral palsy
Mentally handicapped	Person who has learning difficulties

People with disabilities and everyday life

Meeting the needs of people with disabilities

Having a physical or mental impairment need not prevent a disabled person from being able to participate in everyday activities, provided that society supplies them with the special equipment and facilities that they need and does not discriminate against them.

Transport and access in your area

In groups

1 How easy is it for people with disabilities to use public transport in your area? For example, how accessible are your local bus, tube and railway stations to wheelchair users? Are there any buses and trains which are specially designed so that wheelchair users can get on and off them easily?

List any suggestions you have about what could be done to make it easier for people with disabilities to travel on public transport in your area.

2 How easy is it for people with disabilities to get in and around the buildings in your area? Talk about all the places you go to – your school, shops and supermarkets, the cinema, the youth club, the library, the sports centre, the health centre, cafés. If you were in a wheelchair would you be able to get into the buildings and around them?

For your file

Interview a person with a disability and write an article about them. You could publish all your articles in a booklet.

Meeting the need for mobility

Many people with disabilities have impaired mobility – they cannot move from place to place as easily as able-bodied people can. Today, modern wheelchairs can be designed to suit a person's individual needs. Stair lifts can also be fitted inside a person's home.

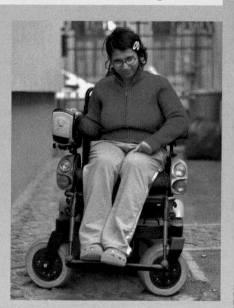

Meeting the need to communicate

Technological developments have revolutionised the lives of many people with severe disabilities. A person who cannot move their limbs and is unable to speak can wear a headband that uses a laser to control a voice synthesiser. The person directs the laser beam at a light-sensitive keyboard. The voice synthesiser then says what they want to say.

Meeting the need for transport

People with impaired mobility have special transport needs. For example, a person with a visual impairment who is travelling by bus or train needs to be informed when their stop is reached. A wheelchair user needs to be able to get their wheelchair onto a bus or a train. Some modern buses have been specially designed with lifts, and modern trains have sliding doors and grab-rails.

Meeting the need for access

People with disabilities may have problems with access if a doorway is not wide enough for a wheelchair or if there are steps or stairs. Lots of older buildings have been altered to widen doors and provide ramps and lifts. New buildings, such as supermarkets, are built with wide aisles and checkouts.

Getting a lot out of life

"People can have a stereotyped view of anyone who's got a disability. They think we can't do things just because we're disabled. How wrong they are..."

Ellie Simmonds of Great Britain with the four swimming medals (2 gold, a silver and a bronze) she won at the Paralympic Games in London.

Ellie was born with a bone growth disorder, which means the bones in her legs are much shorter than average.

Cherry Moore from Belper who was born with Down's Syndrome. She is a talented painter who won a prize aged 15 in a competition which had entries from 1,200 other artists. She has had several one-woman shows and won a number of prizes nationwide.

Alan Oliveira, the Brazilian amputee sprinter, who hopes to take part in both the Olympics and the Paralympics in Rio in 2016.

Some people argue that amputee sprinters should not be allowed to compete in the Olympic Games because their artificial limbs give them an advantage over runners with natural ankles and feet.

Natasha Baker of Great Britain who won two equestrian gold medals at the 2012 Paralympic Games. She cannot feel her legs, so she controls her horse by her voice and upper body movements.

In groups

Talk about people you know with disabilities who have achieved successes, and famous people with disabilities and their achievement, for example former home secretary David Blunkett and wheelchair athlete Tanni Grey-Thompson.

Discuss how much media coverage is given to people with disabilities. Is it true that they are 'largely invisible' because they are under-represented on TV and in newspapers and magazines?

Do you think amputee sprinters should be able to take part in the Olympic Games? Discuss the arguments for and against allowing them to compete.

Reducing waste

Stop talking rubbish,
Start thinking about reducing waste

Derek Johnson explains why we should be concerned about what happens to our waste

Every year we throw away 26 million tonnes of household waste. We are used to putting our bins out each week and to them being emptied. So why is there so much fuss about our rubbish?

The fact is lots of our household waste isn't really rubbish. Look at the piechart that shows what used to be put in the average bin. A lot of these materials can be recycled. That's why many local councils have recycling centres where you can recycle cardboard, paper, plastic and glass.

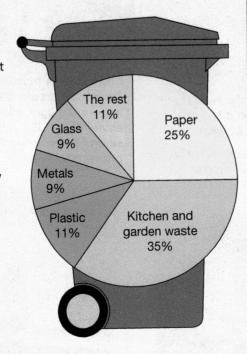

The rest 11%
Glass 9%
Metals 9%
Plastic 11%
Paper 25%
Kitchen and garden waste 35%

Many councils also run kerbside collection schemes whereby you can put recyclable materials in a separate box or wheelie bin. Food waste can be recycled too. It can be put in a separate container and can be used to feed pigs or to generate electricity.

As a result, the proportion of household waste that was recycled in 2010/11 was over 40%. But this was less than in many other European countries: Switzerland, the Netherlands and Germany recycle around 60% of their household waste.

The rest of our rubbish is either dumped in landfill sites or incinerated. In 2010/11, 50% of local authority waste was sent to landfill compared to an EU average of 40%.

Friends of the Earth considers that 80% of our household waste could be recycled or composted. So we've still got a long way to go. Which is why we need to stop talking about rubbish and to do more about reducing waste.

♻ Recycling facts

Glass
Glass jars and bottles could be washed and re-used. Glass can be crushed and recycled, which reduces the amount of raw materials required to make new glass.

Paper
Recycling paper saves trees, because it reduces the amount of wood pulp we have to import to make paper. It also saves on the water and energy used in manufacturing.

Cans
About 600 food and drinks cans are used in a year by each household in the UK. The cans are made of either steel or aluminium, both of which can be recycled. Although aluminium cans have a high scrap value, it is estimated that over 11 million are thrown away in the UK every day.

Plastics
A variety of products can be made from recycled plastics. For example, the plastic used for soft drinks bottles can be re-used as filling inside anoraks and sleeping bags. However, what can be made depends on whether the many different types of plastic are sorted and collected separately.

Organic waste
Organic waste is any waste that is of animal or vegetable origin. A lot of organic waste can be recycled into compost and used as fertiliser on the garden. Some local councils have set up composting schemes and supply composting containers.

Incineration **and** landfill

Most of our waste is burned or buried, which is bad for the environment and our health.

Incineration

The combustion of waste at high temperatures:

- **Encourages more waste**

  Incinerators need a minimum of rubbish to operate. To meet demand, local authorities are abandoning recycling and waste reduction plans.

- **Generates energy inefficiently**

  Incinerators that generate electricity produce more greenhouse gases than gas-fired power stations.

- **Wastes energy**

  Recycling saves far more energy than is generated by burning waste because it means making fewer things from raw materials.

- **Causes pollution**

  Smoke, gases and ash from incinerators can contain harmful dioxins, which are a cause of cancer.

Landfill

Dumping rubbish in the ground or in waste mountains:

- **Releases toxins**

  Rotting rubbish emits explosive gases and polluting liquids. Methane emissions contribute to climate change.

- **Threatens our quality of life**

  Landfill creates problems for local communities. Nuisances include more traffic, noise, odours, smoke, dust, litter and pests.

From bad to worse

European laws are forcing the government to send less waste to landfill and the landfill tax is rising to deter businesses and local authorities from landfilling waste which could be recycled.

The money raised from landfill tax should be used to get our recycling and composting rate as high as other parts of Europe.

> **Friends of the Earth says:**
>
> - **Don't build any more incinerators.**
>
> - **Use money from landfill taxes for recycling and waste reduction.**

In groups

1. Imagine there are plans to build a new waste incinerator in your area. Explain why you would support or oppose the plans.

2. How much of the waste that you produce at home do you recycle? Discuss what you could do at home **a)** to reduce waste **b)** to increase the amount of waste that you recycle. Then share your views in a class discussion.

Role play

In either pairs or groups, plan and act out a sketch involving a character called Wilma Wasteful, who thoughtlessly uses things and then throws them away, and a character called Robin Recycle, who explains what effect Wilma's actions have on the environment and what she can do instead to help him in his war against waste.

For your file

Design a poster to encourage young people to get involved in recycling. Write a short e-mail to a newspaper, explaining 'Why I am concerned about waste.'

Reducing waste at school

Is your school an environmental success or an environmental disaster?

 In pairs

Answer yes or no to the following questions. Add up all the yes answers
to find out if your school deserves praise or needs help urgently.

Classrooms

- Are both sides of paper used for work?
- When photocopying, are the copies double-sided?
- Is there a scrap bin for notes?
- Is paper recycled?
- Are lights turned off when not in use?
- Are computers and whiteboards turned off at the end of the day?

Office/Admin

- Is there a school environmental policy?
- Is recycled paper used for correspondence?
- Is scrap paper re-used?
- Is waste paper recycled?
- Are appliances turned off fully when not in use?
- Are office supplies sourced locally?

Canteen/Kitchen

- Is food sourced locally?
- Are there washable, reusable trays, plates, cups and cutlery?
- Are there recycling bins for cans and glass?
- Is food waste composted?
- Are environmentally friendly products used for cleaning and washing?
- Are cloths used instead of paper towels?
- Are low energy lights used?

Staff Room

- Are tea-bags and coffee grounds composted?
- Are reusable mugs used instead of disposable cups?
- Is water boiled for only those wanting a hot drink?
- Are there recycling bins?
- Are low energy lights used?
- Are lights turned off when the room is empty?

Student Common Rooms

- Is there a person/group responsible for ensuring energy is not wasted?
- Are there recycling bins?

Toilets

- Are there water conservation measures in place?
- Are cloth rolls or air dryers used instead of paper towels?
- Are sensor lights fitted?

Cleaning

- Are environmentally friendly products used for cleaning?
- Are there energy conservation measures in place?
- Is waste minimised?
- Are cleaners encouraged to turn all lights off?

Transport

- Are staff encouraged to car share?
- Are students who could travel by bus discouraged from bringing cars to school?

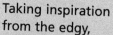

In groups

Study your school's recycling policy. Discuss how well it is implemented. Suggest ways in which you think it could be more effective. For example, are there any materials that are currently thrown away which could be recycled? Is the school saving as much energy as it could?

Read about what the pupils at George Abbot School did to recycle fabrics. Visit your local council's website to find out about its recycling schemes. Discuss what it is doing and whether there is anything your school could do in order to further promote recycling in your area.

How well did your school score?

29–36 You are in an environmentally successful school. Keep looking for more ways to improve and keep up the good work.

22–29 Some good work here but plenty of areas for improvement. Look at all your 'no' answers for the next project to tackle.

15–21 Perhaps you are just starting out? Don't get downhearted – it's worth the effort. Waste reduction and recycling are the easiest to implement.

Less than 15 Definitely could do better! Take it a step at a time and your school can be an environmental success. Turning lights off and reducing waste are good places to start.

Recycling is fashionable at local school

Pupils at George Abbot School in Guildford have been busy transforming rubbish into fashion to celebrate Guildford Borough Council's kerbside collection of textiles.

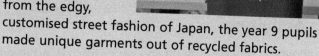

Taking inspiration from the edgy, customised street fashion of Japan, the year 9 pupils made unique garments out of recycled fabrics.

Councillor Jenny Wicks, Lead Councillor for the Environment, said: "It is great to see pupils taking a creative approach to reducing our waste. We collect around 5 tonnes of textiles per month. Cotton and wool produce the greenhouse gas methane in landfill, so recycling textiles is one step towards tackling climate change."

For your file

Write an article for a local newspaper explaining what your school is doing to recycle materials and to save energy, and why you think it is important to do so.

Assessing your progress and achievements

The aim of this unit is to help you to think about what progress you have made and what you have achieved during Year 7. It gives you the chance to discuss your progress with your tutor, to write a statement about your achievements and to look ahead and set yourself targets for what you hope to achieve in Year 8.

Your subjects

Think about the effort you have made in each of your subjects and what your progress and achievements have been.

For example, here is what Dean wrote about his work and progress in Science:

I found writing up the experiments difficult at first, but I understand how to do it now and I've been getting much better grades this term.

For your file

Make a list of all the subjects you are studying and use the five-star system to give yourself grades for effort and progress in each subject:

★★★★★ **excellent**
★★★★ **good**
★★★ **satisfactory**
★★ **poor**
★ **unsatisfactory**

Then write a brief comment on your work and progress in your subjects. Give reasons for the grades you have given yourself, and evidence to support your views of your progress and achievements in each subject.

Your activities

Think about the activities you do and what you have achieved in both school and out-of-school activities.

 In pairs

Each make a list of all the activities you have taken part in this year, both inside and outside school. Include details of events organised by clubs and societies that you belong to, sports activities, drama and musical activities and any school events that you have been involved in.

Show your list to your partner and discuss any events that were particular highlights because of what you achieved in them.

For your file

Write a short statement giving details of your most significant achievements in your activities during the year.

Your skills

Think about your progress in the key skills that you are learning as a result of the work which you do in your different subjects. These are the key skills:

- Communication skills
- Numeracy skills
- Study skills
- Problem-solving skills
- Personal and social skills
- ICT skills

For your file

Study the list of key skills and write a short comment on each one, saying how much you think you have improved that skill during the past year – a lot, quite a lot, or only a little. Support your statement by referring to something you have done during the year.

For example, here's what Sasha wrote about her study skills:

My study skills have improved a lot. I've learned how to pick out the main points when I take notes, rather than just copy everything out.

Your attitude and behaviour

Think about what your attitude and behaviour have been like during the year.

- Have your attendance and punctuality been good?
- Has your behaviour been good: **a)** in lessons; **b)** around the school?
- Have you kept up-to-date with your work and handed it in on time?
- Have you volunteered for things, and played as full a part as you could in the life of the school?

For your file

Write a short comment summing up your attitude and behaviour during Year 7.

Discussing your progress

Arrange a meeting with your tutor. Show them what you have written about yourself and discuss your progress and achievements in your subjects and in developing your key skills. Compare your own views with those that your teachers have made on subject reports or subject review sheets during the course of the year. Together decide what your strengths and weaknesses are at present.

Talk about the activities in which you have taken part and what you consider to be your significant achievements, and discuss what you wrote about your attitude and behaviour.

During the meeting, listen carefully to what your tutor has to say. Add anything to your statements which your tutor thinks you have missed out. Note down any comments they make in which they disagree with your assessment, either because they think you have been too harsh on yourself, or because they think that you have overestimated the amount of progress you have made.

Recording your achievements

Use a word processor program to draft a statement as a record of your progress and achievements during Year 7. Include comments on your subjects, your key skills, your activities and your attitude and behaviour.

Before you put the record in your progress file, show it to your tutor. Agree any changes that your tutor thinks you should make, so that your final statement is what you both consider to be an accurate record of your progress and achievements.

Setting targets

You can also use your meeting with your tutor to set targets for the future. Assessing what has gone well can help you to identify which subjects and skills you need to improve. When you have identified a subject or a skill that you need to improve, you can set yourself a target and draw up an action plan.

Think about the comments you have written about your subjects and your skills. Decide which skills and subjects you would most like to try to improve in Year 8. Discuss with your tutor what you would have to do and the things you would have to change in order to improve in that subject or skill.

Index

Acknowledgments

The publishers wish to thank the following for permission to reproduce text. Every effort has been made to trace copyright holders and to obtain their permission for the use of copyright materials. The publishers will gladly receive any information enabling them to rectify any error or omission at the first opportunity.

p7 'Manjit's Story' adapted from *The Facts about…Fears and Phobias* by Renardo Barden, Hodder & Stoughton Ltd, p9 'Packing up your cares and woes' from *Feeling Great* by Vickie Bramwell, published by Piccadilly Press, text ©Vickie Bramwell, 1996, p11 'Becoming a man' adapted from *How Sex Works* by Elizabeth Fenwick and Richard Walker, Dorling Kindersley, p24 'The Right Thing?' from *Red, White and Blue* by Robert Leeson © HarperCollins*Publishers*, p27 'Table manners' adapted from 'Polite society' by Mary Edwards, *Guardian Education*, 28 Oct 1997 © *The Guardian*, p28 'I need my own space' adapted from *Shout*, issue 95 © D.C. Thomson & Co. Ltd, reproduced with kind permission of D.C. Thomson & Co. Ltd, on behalf of Shout Magazine, p30 extract based on 'Top sneaky tips on how to get on with your family better' from 'The Cheat's Guide to Parents' from *Shout*, issue 116 © D.C. Thomson & Co. Ltd, reproduced with kind permission of D.C. Thomson & Co. Ltd, on behalf of Shout Magazine, p31 'Getting on with brothers and sisters' adapted from *Shout*, issue 107 © D.C. Thomson & Co. Ltd, reproduced with kind permission of D.C. Thomson & Co. Ltd, on behalf of Shout Magazine, p33 'The high costs of smoking' adapted from *Youth Topics*, issue 16 produced by CAFOD, used with permission, p34 'What do you really think about smoking?' adapted from *Taking Breath* © the Health Education Authority, p39 'Teenagers Issued With Ban' adapted from *Burnley Express*, 25 February 2013, p40 'What is Bullying?' from www.yourteenlife.co.uk website, North Essex NHS, p44 Stay SMART online from Childnet – www.childnet.com, p44 'How to Beat the Bullies' from *Shout*, issue 105 © D.C. Thomson & Co. Ltd, reproduced with kind permission of D.C. Thomson & Co. Ltd, on behalf of Shout Magazine, p44 'Dealing with taunts and insults' from *You Can Beat Bullying* © Kidscape, 2 Grosvenor Gardens, London, SW1 ODH. We would like to thank the anti-bullying charity Kidscape for their support, and permission to use this extract, p49 'The hero's point of view' from *The Media: What's the Big Idea?* by Belinda Hollyer © Hodder & Stoughton Ltd, p54 'Your Rights at Home' from *Young Citizen's Passport – Your Guide to the Law*, Hodder & Stoughton Ltd, p59 extract from 'Factsheet on Child Labour', produced by CAFOD, reproduced with permission, p59 'Sawai's story' from New Internationalist, July 1997 © *New Internationalist*, p67 'Sammy's statement' adapted from *The User* by Aidan Macfarlane, Magnus Macfarlane and Philip Robson, used with the permission of Oxford University Press, p67 'Fay's problem' adapted from *Shout*, Issue 105 © D.C. Thomson & Co. Ltd, reproduced with kind permission of D.C. Thomson & Co. Ltd, on behalf of Shout Magazine, p73 'Who influences what you buy?' adapted from 'Making Consumer Choices', Trading Standards Institute, p74 'What are my rights?' adapted from 'What is a consumer?', Trading Standards Institute, p75 'Consumer Protection Laws' adapted from 'What is a consumer?', Trading Standards Institute, p77 'Should battery cages be banned?' from 'Ban the Battery Cage', Compassion in World Farming, p77 'Battery hens 'as happy as birds that can roam outside" is from 'As happy as birds that can roam outside' by Ben Farmer, from *Mail Online*, 15 July 2007, reproduced with permission of Solo Syndication, p 82–85 extracts from *The Usbourne Book of Food, Fitness and Health* by Judy Tatchell, reproduced with permission of Usbourne Publishing, 83–85 Saffron Hill, London EC1N 8RT, p88 What is constitutional Monarchy? From *The British Monarchy* website;, p98 'What is a disability?' from *What Do You Know About People With Disabilities?*, P. Sanders and S. Myers ©Aladdin Books Limited, p98 'Becoming disabled' from What Do You Know About People With Disabilities?, P. Sanders and S. Myers ©Aladdin Books Limited, p99 extract from Activity 1 in 'Youth Topics No.18 – Disability', CAFOD, p99 extracts from 'What it's like to be me', compiled by Helen Exley © Helen Exley, Exley Publications Ltd, p101 'Down's girl is honoured with a show of her own' from *The Daily Mail*, 20 Oct 1999, reproduced with permission from Solo Syndication, p103 'Incineration and landfill' used with kind permission from Friends of the Earth, p104 extract adapted from 'Is your school an environmental success or an environmental disaster?', West Wales Eco Centre, p105 extract from 'Recycling is fashionable at local school', Guildford Borough Council.

The publishers wish to thank the following for permission to reproduce photographs. Every effort has been made to trace copyright holders and to obtain their permission for the use of copyright materials. The publishers will gladly receive any information enabling them to rectify any error or omission at the first opportunity.

(t = top, c = centre, b = bottom, r = right, l = left)

Cover & p1 Shariff Che Lah/Dreamstime, p6 Monkey Business Images/Shutterstock, p7 v.s.anandhakrishna/Shutterstock, p8 Golden Pixels LLC/Shutterstock, p9 Iakov Filimonov/Shutterstock, p10 Fabiana Ponzi/Shutterstock, p11 Creatista/Shutterstock, p12 Ollyy/Shutterstock, p14 Monkey Business Images/Shutterstock, p15 Trinity Mirror Publishing, p16 Nir Levy/Shutterstock, p17 Danish Siddiquil/Reuters/Corbis, p18 Monkey Business Images/Shutterstock, p19 bikeriderlondon/Shutterstock, p20 YanLev/Shutterstock, p22t Gina Buliga/Shutterstock, p22b sunsetman/Shutterstock, p24 Monkey Business Images/Shutterstock, p25 stester/Shutterstock, p26 Alexander Raths/Shutterstock, p28 Blend Images/Caroline Schiff/Getty Images, p29 Catherine Murray/Shutterstock, p30 asife/Shutterstock, p31t Gelpi JM/Shutterstock, p31b DNF Style/Shutterstock, p32 Valentyna Chukhlyebova/Shutterstock, p33 Gajus/Shutterstock, p34 Syda Productions/Shutterstock, p35t scyther5/Shutterstock, p35b mkmakingphotos/Shutterstock, p36–37 David Tipling/Oxford Scientific/Getty Images, p38t LeeAnn White/Shutterstock, p38b Eldad Carin/Shutterstock, p39 Alan Bailey/Shutterstock, p40l JStone/Shutterstock, p40r Featureflash/Shutterstock, p41 Digital Media Pro/Shutterstock, p42 wrangler/Shutterstock, p43 Helder Almeida/Shutterstock, p45 oliveromg/Shutterstock, p46 EJWhite/Shutterstock, p47 Featureflash/Shutterstock, p48t The Washington Post/Getty Images, p48b guentermanaus/Shutterstock, p49l 1000 Words/Shutterstock, p49r Sadik Gulec/Shutterstock, p50 absolute-india/Shutterstock, p54t with thanks to ChildLine, p54b Galina Barskaya/Shutterstock, p56t draganica/Shutterstock, p56c MJTH/Shutterstock, p56b jdwfoto/Shutterstock, p57 DNF Style/Shutterstock, p58 Mila Supinskaya/Shutterstock, p59 Sam Dcruz/Shutterstock, p60 tehcheesiong/Shutterstock, p61 Orange Line Media/Shutterstock, p62 Adam Gilchrist/Shutterstock, p63t Kiev.Victor/Shutterstock, p63c Courtesy of The Advertising Archives, p63b Courtesy of The Advertising Archives, p64 Africa Studio/Shutterstock, p65 bikeriderlondon/Shutterstock, p66 Photographee.eu/Shutterstock, p67 J. Henning Buchholz/Shutterstock, p68 Iakov Filimonov/Shutterstock, p69 Donjiy/Shutterstock, p70l mikecphoto/Shutterstock, p70r Daniel Gale/Shutterstock, p71 mangostock/Shutterstock, p72l Kzenon/Shutterstock, p72r Smiltena/Shutterstock, p73 Monkey Business Images/Shutterstock, p74 westernstudio/Shutterstock, p75 Racorn/Shutterstock, p76 tmcphotos/Shutterstock, p77 krugloff/Shutterstock, p78 Matej Hudovernik/Shutterstock, p79 michaeljung/Shutterstock, p80 Samuel Borges Photography/Shutterstock, p82 wavebreakmedia/Shutterstock, p83 ZouZou/Shutterstock, p84t BlueOrange Studio/Shutterstock, p84b jordache/Shutterstock, p85 Ferdaus Shamim/WireImage/Getty Images, p86 Jeff Overs/BBC News & Current Affairs/Getty Images, p86–87 Tutti Frutti/Shutterstock, p88 Featureflash/Shutterstock, p89t Lisa S/Shutterstock, p89c Duirinish Light/Shutterstock, p89b Matthew Dixon/Shutterstock, p90 Sylvie Poggio Artists, p91t Pressmaster/Shutterstock, p91b Janine Wiedel/Photolibrary/Alamy, p92 wavebreakmedia/Shutterstock, p93t dgdimension/Shutterstock, p93c g-stockstudio/Shutterstock, p93b Khakimullin Aleksandr/Shutterstock, p96 Stefano Tinti/Shutterstock, p97 karelnoppe/Shutterstock, p98 photomak/Shutterstock, p99t Stokkete/Shutterstock, p99c Denis Kuvaev/Shutterstock, p99b Jaren Jai Wicklund/Shutterstock, p100 Marcel Jancovic/Shutterstock, p101tl Tom Dulat/Stringer/Getty Images, p101tr Page One Press Agency, p101bl Julian Finney/Getty Images, p101br Julian Finney/Getty Images, p102tt Africa Studio/Shutterstock, p102t Tim Masters/Shutterstock, p102c Nuttapong Wongcheronkit/Shutterstock, p102b Yeko Photo Studio/Shutterstock, p102bb audaxl/Shutterstock, p103 schab/Shutterstock, p105 AVAVA/Shutterstock, p107 Monkey Business Images/Shutterstock.